"Carole Goodwin's love for Quicksilvers' really comes through in this book; and that is, after all, what it takes to be successful with early adolescents. Next, you need an absolutely accurate understanding of who these kids are. This book will give it to you. I think I've met most of the kids Carole profiles in her book. She is a keen observer of adolescent culture. Every youth worker will benefit from her perspective and wisdom. A welcome addition to any youth worker's resource library!"

Wayne Rice
Editor, *Youthworker*

"*Quicksilvers: Ministering with Junior High Youth* is a wonderful blend of experience and theory. Considering my 10 years of ministry with junior high on a parish level and three years on a diocesan level, I think Carole Goodwin is right on target. The book will not only prove useful to those with experience to know theory and how it relates to their experiences, but will also be especially insightful to new people working with junior high youth. I would highly recommend it for anyone working in this ministry."

Nancy Housh
Director of Youth and Young Adult Ministry
Archdiocese of Oklahoma City

"In *Quicksilvers: Ministering with Junior High Youth*, Carole Goodwin does a wonderful job of inviting us into the world of young adolescents. Her portrait of young adolescents is both compassionate and realistic—a much needed antidote to the many stereotypes about young adolescents. The combination of insights and practical directions will assist leaders to more effectively minister with young adolescents."

John Roberto
Director, Center for Youth Ministry Development

"The important dialogue about the whys, wherefores, and how-tos of ministry with young adolescents in the 1990s is just emerging. Carole Goodwin's book contributes to this investigation and dialogue. Written with a conversational and imaginative voice, this book offers practical insights and suggestions from which both parents and youth ministers should benefit. I especially like the many stories about young adolescents and about actual ministry experiences that Carole includes in her work."

Butch Ekstrom
Center for Youth Ministry Development

"Carole Goodwin blends a clear understanding of early adolescents with a clear grasp of the 'vision of youth ministry.' *Quicksilvers* is filled with stories of 'real' adolescents dealing with real concerns and issues. Goodwin weaves solid theory on adolescents' personal and faith development with practical strategies and approaches for effective ministry with this age group.

"For those experienced in youth ministry, *Quicksilvers* is very useful as a concise resource on early adolescent ministry. It is invaluable for those new to early adolescent ministry, and is wonderful reading for parents! It is gratifying to see someone rooted in parish ministry and involved in the day-to-day lives of early adolescents write so sensitively about young people."

Robert J. McCarthy
Office of Youth Ministry
Archdiocese of Baltimore

"*Quicksilvers* is brimming with potential for educating parents and others in the needs of this age group. It uses very effective stories to highlight the developmental needs of youth. It is clear in its message of the need for better parish awareness and understanding of the Quicksilver years. I will recommend it to my new religious education director and those who will be working with this age group."

Rev. Joseph Felker
Pastor, Sacred Heart Church
Redlands, California

*Foreword by Thomas H. Groome*

# Quicksilvers

## Ministering with Junior High Youth

### CAROLE GOODWIN

TWENTY-THIRD PUBLICATIONS
Mystic, Connecticut 06355

Twenty-Third Publications
185 Willow Street
P.O. Box 180
Mystic CT 06355
(203) 536-2611
800-321-0411

© Copyright 1992 Carole Goodwin. All rights reserved. No part of this publication may be reproduced in any manner without prior written permission of the publisher. Write to Permissions Editor.

ISBN 0-89622-519-4
Library of Congress Catalog Card Number 92-81798

# Foreword

*Ministry to the "Lost and Found"*

Young adolescence is the area of life when people are most likely to experience a deep sense of being lost, and likewise the time that holds the most possibility for beginning to find their own "selves."

Developmentalists advise that this phase of life is typically marked by a "conventional" perspective on faith, morals, social awareness, and so on. This means that young adolescents are likely to function according to the dictates of what "they" say, with a perspective more followed than chosen, more from outside than from within. Herein lies both the hazard of their becoming "lost," and likewise the possibility of them beginning to "come to themselves." Remember the young prodigal in the gospel; it is when he "comes to himself" (Luke 15:17), that he can leave the "far country."

The possibility of young adolescents getting lost, sometimes with permanent and tragic consequences, arises from what Kierkegaard called "the dizziness of choice" they face between competing "authorities." They have moved beyond the affiliative time of childhood (in Fowler's terms, stage 2 of faith development) when the authority of parents or guardians was typically accepted, or at least not ultimately questioned. Now, as their worlds broaden in early adolescence, they may have myriad authorities, all of them with a powerful attraction and many pointing in competing directions.

On the other hand, by the very fact of having to confront real choices, this era holds the possibility of a breakthrough in their discernment and decision making toward their own best selves. A crucial variable in whether or not young adolescents get permanently "lost or found" is the kind of adult sponsorship they have for negotiating this most hazardous crossing-over in life's journey. And surely a Christian faith community has a serious responsibility to be "with" its young adolescents in concerted and competent ministry at this time in life. This brings us to the worthiness of this small but very powerful book.

Carole Goodwin offers a gem here to all who are involved with or concerned about the church's pastoral response to young adolescents. Carole has made a life-work out of ministry to her beloved "Quicksilvers" as she calls them, potentially lost and found young people whose personalities, from an adult perspective at least, may often seem to have the fluidity of mercury. The deep empathy, great sensitivity, abiding hospitality, and compassionate understanding with which she writes are clearly born of memory, of experience, of well informed theory, of imagination, and especially of a loving heart. Her style is engaging and non-technical, her suggestions are practical and imaginative; this is a "user friendly" book!

Carole Goodwin weaves together here an engaging conversation between her own experience of working with "Quicksilvers" and her extensive knowledge of the theoretical literature that might throw light on her concern; I would call it a dialogue between theory and praxis, always essential to good ministry. Her thoughts and proposals are well informed by the latest social science research and by theological and philosophical considerations. Yet, her reflections also uncover the wisdom from her own experience, and the text is interlaced with very helpful stories about young teenagers that illustrate and illuminate her insights. This conversational style invites readers to join in the dialogue and to add their own "word" to it from their journey and work "with" young adolescents in ministry. Readers will emerge from this dialogue with a better sense, even if they have a good one already, of how to minister with early adolescents. What more could any one book do?

Thomas H. Groome<br>
Professor of Theology and Religious Education<br>
Boston College

## Dedication

To my parents who patiently nurtured my own
Quicksilver years

To the Quicksilvers in my life who have allowed
me to become a companion on their journeys of faith

To Dave who taught me to appreciate the joys of
youth ministry

# Contents

Foreword by Thomas H. Groome — *v*

Introduction — 1

1. Developmental Characteristics — 4
   Who Are Quicksilvers?

2. Foundational Elements for Ministry — 23
   How Should We Minister with Them?

3. Self, Family, Friends, School, Media — 34
   What Stresses and Pressures Are on Quicksilvers?

4. Self-Esteem, Substance Abuse, Sexuality, Suicide — 51
   What Critical Issues Do Quicksilvers Face?

5. Evangelization: Invitation, Catechesis, Conversion — 69
   How Do Quicksilvers Grow in Faith?

Conclusion — 84

# Introduction

Twenty years ago I was invited by a good friend, Dave Imming, to help with a high school weekend retreat. I remember being a little nervous about spending 48 hours with adolescents. I had always avoided teenagers because I was certain that the cliches I had heard were true. They are rebellious, hard to handle, argumentative. They never sleep! They don't trust anyone over 21! That weekend changed not only my perception of teenagers; it also completely changed the focus of my life and ministry. I learned to appreciate the energy that young people bring to life. I learned that young people are compassionate, curious about life, and genuinely hungry for opportunities to discuss where and how God interacts with humanity. I also learned that, true to the stereotype, teenagers do not sleep; but I saw they truly love being with adults and often minister to each other in ways adults would never dream of.

My ministry to young people has grown considerably since that first weekend of no sleep and close encounters with God! Since then I have been invited into the lives of many young people across the United States and I hope I have been able, through workshop presentations and writing, to touch the lives of countless others.

Most of the young people who have directly graced my ministry are from the south central part of this country. I work in parish and diocesan youth ministry in Oklahoma, which seems to me to represent a microcosm of adolescent concerns, issues, problems and joys.

Eleven years ago, I was invited to do a short presentation at a diocesan catechist meeting on junior high ministry. I searched frantically for information and resources on or about this age group. My search was futile. There were no manuals, programs, no advice on how to go about ministering to this apparently forgotten age group. I began collecting bits and pieces of information and ideas, and have since been able to concentrate my own research and ministerial dreams on this age group. The majority of workshops I have conducted in the past few years have dealt with youth ministry issues that particularly impact the lives of younger adolescents.

This book is a response to the expressed need of ministers in the field of youth ministry who work with young people between the ages of 10 and 16. I call those in this age group "Quicksilvers." Quicksilver literally means "living fluidity" and refers to the metal, mercury. Anyone who has stepped into a junior-high classroom has been privileged to witness first-hand this behavior of a unique developmental stage of life! The term "quicksilver" was coined by the Search Institute to describe the time of life between childhood and high school, the least-studied age group and for whom the least amount of creative religious teaching materials is available. As a result, people in youth ministry continually express that their greatest professional needs are for information, ideas, and theoretical grounding for their work among Quicksilvers.

One of my own early needs motivated the writing of this book. Nowhere to my knowledge was there a collection of information for ministers and leaders that dealt with the unique developmental characteristics, personal needs, crisis issues, and faith concerns of young adolescents. In addition, in my travels and workshop sites, I discovered that many of the people who are doing youth ministry have not had opportunities to investigate the theoretical principles that give this important field a solid grounding.

In this book, then, I am attempting to weave my own experiences with the theory that undergirds my ministry. I identify the foundational principles that were designed by the National Federation for Catholic Youth Ministry as the theoretical grounding for ministry with youth. I also review key elements of the youth subculture and issues that affect young people's lives.

I share many stories from the lives of actual young people. These are stories of youth who have been a part of my life and enriched my ministry. I have also cited information from interviews with Quicksilvers I have held in the past eight years. Every young person named in this book is real, but names and sometimes the specific details of their lives have been changed. I have done this to save them embarrassment, but I would like to thank them nevertheless for their honesty and willingness to share their pain and joy with me and my readers.

I still regard ministry to adolescents as a challenge, but not in the same way I did 20 years ago. Today I see the challenge as one that calls for a recognition that Quicksilvers are in a unique time of life. It is a time that should be celebrated and honored with programming and attention that is sensitive to their natural restlessness, their need for experiences of independence, and their need for opportunities to relate to their God in new and different ways.

I want to particularly thank the young people of St. Gregory's Parish in Enid, Oklahoma. Many of their individual stories are blended into the stories you will read here. They are an important part of my story and I offer both their stories and my experience in a form I hope will challenge you as you attempt to minister to the Quicksilvers in your own lives.

Chapter 1

*Who Are Quicksilvers?*

# Developmental Characteristics

I often spend time in the homes of families as a part of my parish ministry. I love being a part of the day-to-day lives of the young people I work with. An interesting phenomenon I have observed is that when a child is an infant or toddler, parents and significant others "celebrate" each developmental change. Parents make countless long-distance calls to share the news that the child has learned to turn over, has mastered the intricacies of feeding himself or herself, and has attempted a variety of life skills that signify growing up.

Amazingly enough, parents proudly note even "negative" behaviors as milestones in development. They recognize temper tantrums and saying "No!" as normal, and consider uncontrolled egocentricity "cute."

The same parents dread the behavioral changes in adolescence that parallel these earlier characteristics. Young adolescents frequently receive the message: "You are less than wonderful, and we can't wait until you have outgrown this phase!" Teachers, parents, and other adults in the community often make comments that reinforce this attitude. All of this would lead us to believe that Quicksilvers are among the most disliked, misunderstood, and least tolerated age group around. It's no wonder that self-esteem is one of the greatest problems they face.

In all areas of life Quicksilvers are experiencing change. Physical, cognitive, emotional, social, moral, identity search, and faith development changes have strongly identifiable characteristics in these quicksilver years. When we recognize these characteristics, we come to a greater understanding of their normalcy in the life journey of these young people.

Theorists have written volumes on adolescent development, but I have found it extremely difficult to find information that specifically deals with Quicksilvers. Assuming that you have a similar problem, I have attempted to put together here a capsuled look at the developmental characteristics unique to Quicksilvers to give you a clearer understanding of expected behaviors for this time of life. I will lean heavily on information from the developmentalists, but I will also share conversations I have had with Quicksilvers themselves.

**Don't Pigeon-Hole People**
First, however, I would like to offer the following caution. We often pigeon-hole people when we talk about stages of development. When we do this we fail to recognize the uniqueness of each and every individual.

> There is no more widely variable group that we can deal with than adolescents, especially young adolescents. Because of this extreme variability, there can be a six year span in biological development between a quickly developing girl and a slowly developing boy, and here I am talking only about biological age. To think about all the "ages" that an adolescent juggles—biological, social, emotional, intellectual and academic—makes a mockery of chronological age. To be told that someone is 13 is to be told just about

nothing about the person. This one characteristic of adolescence, especially early adolescents—its variability—poses the greatest challenge to service providers.[1]

With this caution in mind, let's investigate the following developmental tasks of early adolescence: puberty, personality, moral, and faith development. These will give us a quick picture of the identifiable characteristics common to these young people.

Young people experience the most rapid physiological changes in their lives since infancy somewhere between the ages of 10 and 16. These abrupt physical changes tend to cause emotional unrest and mark the onset of the biological period called puberty.

In recent years, our knowledge of the human reproductive system and organ function has helped us gain better understanding of the bodily changes in puberty. In females, the sequence is 1) changes in hormonal balance, 2) beginning of skeletal growth, 3) beginning of breast development, 4) appearance of straight pigmented pubic hair, 5) maximum growth spurt, 6) appearance of kinky, pigmented pubic hair, 7) first menstruation and appearance of darkened hair on forearms and hair on underarms.

In males the sequence is 1) changes in hormonal balance, 2) beginning of skeletal growth, 3) the enlargement of the genitals, 4) the appearance of straight pigmented pubic hair, 5) early voice change, 6) first ejaculation, 7) appearance of kinky, pigmented pubic hair, 8) maximum growth spurt, 9) appearance of downy facial hair, 10) appearance of hair on chest and forearms, 11) late voice change, and 12) coarse pigmented facial hair.[2]

Given our understanding of the physiology of adolescents and the differences in individuals and cultures, we can conclude that no single event marks the onset of puberty. Rather each person experiences a series of sequential physical changes that places him or her in this complex phase of growth, or development.

Current research is sparse on the effect of puberty on a youngster's self-image and his or her relationships with peers. When we listen to what the young people themselves say, we can easily identify this stage of life as one that contains a critical developmental crisis.

The following was asked of high school students who were interviewed for this study:[3]

> Puberty is the time when your body begins to change and you begin to resemble an adult physically. Describe your body (height, weight, and changes). Tell how you feel about your body (and those changes). How have those changes affected your relationships with your friends? If you are well into puberty, describe what it was like when you first began to change physically. If you have not begun to change physically, describe the feelings you have about yourself, especially any fears you have. Describe how other kids treat you.

The young people who answered these questions were all 15 years old when they responded.

When I was 11, just before sixth grade, I spent the summer with my grandparents. That began the worst year of my life. I grew everywhere. I grew three inches taller, grew breasts and had my first period. I was embarrassed to go home again. I didn't want any of my friends to see me. I was afraid for school to start again. I just knew my friends would think I looked like a freak. I was right! The other girls started avoiding me at recess. My mother said the other girls were just jealous, but that didn't make me feel any better.

The only good thing was that the eighth-grade boys seemed to pay more attention to me. That made me feel a little better, but I was lonesome for girlfriends, someone to talk to. I just wish I had

been older when all this happened to me. I hated being different.
—Sara

I am 15 years old and in the ninth grade. I am 4' 9" tall and weigh 87 pounds and have no body hair. I hate P.E., especially the locker room. I am the smallest kid in class. One of our requirements is to bench press 100 pounds. I laughed when the teacher told us that. I don't even weigh 100 pounds. The coach laughed when I told him there was no way I could do that. The other kids make fun of me all the time. I wish I was still in junior high. At least there are some other kids my size there. I hate my body. The thing I am the most afraid of is that I will look like this the rest of high school. —Larry

Sometimes I worry that something is wrong with me. I'm flat, short and haven't had my period yet. I look like a kid and the boys pay no attention to me. All my friends have boyfriends or at least get asked out on dates. My parents say I can date when I am 16. I'm afraid that that will make no difference because no one will ask out a baby. (That's what the kids in gym call me.) I don't know what to do. My mom says if I'm bothered that much maybe I should talk to the doctor. With my luck the doctor would probably say I am just perfect for a 10 year old! I can't wait for puberty. I just hope I don't break records for the oldest person to reach normal growth! —Teresa

I guess I'm pretty normal. I'm tall but I have always been big for my age. I've been shaving since the 8th grade and am 6' 2" and weigh 180 pounds. I have always been good at sports and am one of the back-up quarterbacks on the high school team. I have a lot of friends and I think I am pretty popular. I'm not bragging, but I am glad that I am big and strong. —Marcus

I guess you could say that I am average. My body is okay, although I wish I was bigger and heavier. I am 5' 5" tall and I weigh about 145 pounds. I'm too small for football or basketball, but I am going out for tennis and track. Those are the sports that count at our school. It's important if you want to be popular to be on one of those teams. The biggest thing is I have an early birthday, so I'll get my license before my friends do. That will help my popularity!  —Jake

I guess I am lucky. I'm pretty satisfied with my looks. I am a cheerleader so I get plenty of exercise and I am automatically accepted by everyone. I try not to be snobby and am friendly to everyone, even the nerdy kids. I think it's important for school leaders to be friendly with everyone.

As far as puberty, I don't remember any problems. I grew and developed about the same time as my friends and my mom always talked to me about what was happening. My mom did a really neat thing; she sent me a rose the day after I had my first period. The card said: "Congratulations, you are growing up."  —Lisa

These anecdotes are examples of typical feelings for early, late and average maturers among the 75 fifteen year olds who were surveyed. I do not cite these anecdotes as examples of scientific norms, but as representative of the feelings expressed by those 75 young people.

### Puberty Affects Self-Esteem

Despite a great variability in adolescent growth, we should keep in mind that self-image and peer relationships are not entirely determined by physical maturity. Pubertal changes can, however, affect peer approval and the development of a strong self-image.

Females who physically mature early often feel alienated from peers, especially other females. A typical young woman in this position tends to feel conspicuous and vulnerable. She often experiences negative feelings about herself because she looks different from her age mates. Generally her feelings of self-dissatisfaction decrease as her age mates begin to experience pubertal changes and their physical differences lessen.

Late maturers, both male and female, are usually at a distinct disadvantage in terms of popularity and self-esteem. Typically they are the "locker room scapegoats" or the class clowns. They tend to engage in all types of compensating behavior which further isolates them from their more mature peers. They look like younger children, tend to identify with and behave like younger children, and therefore are treated as such by both peers and significant adults.

On the other hand, the male who physically matures early is regarded with respect and envy by his male peers. His female peers are in constant attendance and he is the object of their continual ploys for attention. A young person who enjoys advanced physical size and good coordination usually has athletic talents. For a male, this has long meant automatic popularity in our culture. A typical young man in this position usually enjoys a positive self-image and is successful in most of his endeavors. He is often a school leader and gets along well with his peers and adults. Possibly the only disadvantage for him is that he is under the constant pressure of high expectations from adults.

Average maturers do not appear to have problems with self-regard or popularity with peers. Both males and females in this position have the advantage of less stress in their development. They do not have to deal with feelings of inadequacy or the pressures of unreal expectations that permeate the lives of the early or late maturers.

Puberty is not a gentle growth period linking childhood to adolescence. Rather it is the struggle young people face as they journey through adolescence to maturity. Some, as the following story illustrates, have extraordinary obstacles to overcome.

### A Story about Jeff, age 15

His name is Jeff. He is 15 years old and he lives by himself. He has a mattress, a sleeping bag, a TV and a small lamp for his furniture. His clothes are kept in a box by the TV. He also owns a bicycle and a lawnmower. His 27-year-old sister signed the lease for him and he eats his evening meal with her, her three children and her fiance.

He moved to our town last summer when his newly-married mother and fourth stepfather kicked him out of their lives. He hitch-hiked through three states to come to his sister. He found out that she was not able to take him in, but she found him a two-room apartment and paid for the utility hook-ups and two months rent.

Jeff goes to school. His sister is listed as his guardian. He also works at a local fast-food restaurant for minimum wage. (He lied about his age.) To supplement his income, he plans to find as many mowing jobs as possible this summer. He is just able to pay his bills and he hopes to increase his work hours to save for a car.

Jeff met with me at his sister's request because he constantly fights with her fiance. She is afraid she will have to ask Jeff to stop coming for dinner if the fighting does not stop.

"He's a jerk," Jeff relates. "He thinks if he marries her he can take over my life too! He tells me my grades are too low, that I should be more responsible, that education is my key to success. He's always on my back because I never have money and have to borrow from her. He doesn't know anything about me!" Jeff's anger and frustration began to become more obvious as he paced around my office. "He's just like every other adult who gets their kicks out of putting me down," Jeff continued. "My teachers ride me for not working up to my potential, and yesterday my boss said if I was late once more my job was in jeopardy. They're all a bunch of jerks! They don't care about me, even though they all say they do. I don't trust any of them!" With that Jeff broke down into a wave of tears that signified his overwhelming despair.

I looked with sadness at this man-child who has been forced to leave childhood and to skip adolescence long before he is ready to move into adulthood and its responsibilities. His unusual circumstances are not uncommon in today's society.

## Turning Points in Development

Erik Erikson identifies eight conflicts in life that need some resolution in order for a person to develop a healthy personality. In addition, he names eight virtues that are gained when one comes to a successful resolution of each conflict. Erikson considers the resolutions "turning points" in development.

We will look at Erikson's description of five of these conflicts to determine how they are useful in our attempt to gain a deeper understanding of Quicksilvers. Erikson says we meet these conflicts initially in childhood and we understand their importance to our self-knowledge as their successful or unsuccessful resolution impacts our ego strength and personality in adulthood.

In infancy (0-2 years of age), we learn to react to our relationships and our environment with either trust or mistrust. If our basic needs are met, we adopt trust as our normal behavioral stance. The virtue we thus gain is that of "hope." This stage is a grounding for future comfort in our relationships with other people. The successful resolution of its conflict also helps us to respond to God with an attitude of hopefulness and to respond to life as basically good.

As we progress into the world of the toddler (2-3 years of age), we become assertive and learn the virtue of "will." We resolve the conflict between autonomy and shame/self-doubt. We grow in self-esteem when we are accepted unconditionally, even when our resounding favorite word is "No"!

As we journey from childhood through adolescence into adulthood, autonomy is the action that allows us to separate our identity from that of our caregivers. It becomes a continual task of life throughout adulthood. We experience individuation and are able to stand apart from significant others when we successfully resolve this conflict. We acknowledge our own worth and recognize our right to recognition and attention.

We meet the conflict of initiative versus guilt between the ages of three and five. We struggle to initiate actions and plans on our own and to discover that at times we do not meet the expectations of the adults in our lives. A successful resolution of this conflict empowers us to follow our own dreams and desires and to align these within the confines of our caregivers' expectations. Erikson claims this is the time of life when conscience begins and the virtue gained in this stage is "purpose."

In the elementary school years (ages 6 to 12), we learn to master skills and gain confidence in our ability to accomplish tasks. When a lack of life stability hinders our acquisition of skills, we are often left with feelings of inferiority. Successful resolution of the conflict between industry versus inferiority leaves us with the virtue of "competence." This builds our self-esteem and helps us to eradicate feelings of inferiority. This stage is a crucial one for adolescents.

The teenage years (13-18) are the years that Erikson identifies as those for resolving the conflict between identity and role diffusion. We test our self-understanding against how others regard us. As we identify our talents and dreams about our potential roles, we begin to image our "self" as an important contributor to the future. We search for causes and devote ourselves to their completion. We are ready to make commitments and gain the virtue of "fidelity."[4]

Erikson's fifth stage has come under new discussion among those who work with adolescents.

> We have identified one period of adolescence that begins with the onset of puberty and ends with graduation from high school. The "early" stage of adolescence is characterized by rapid physical changes, significant conceptual maturation, and heightened sensitivity to peer approval. We have called the psychosocial crisis of this period group identity versus alienation. The second or later stage of adolescence begins at approximately 18 years of age and continues for about three or four years. This stage is characterized by the attainment of autonomy from the family and the development of a sense of personal identity. We have

called the psychosocial crisis of this period individual identity versus role diffusion. The second adolescent stage closely parallels Erikson's conceptualization of the entire period of adolescence.

While we agree that the crisis of personal identity accurately reflects the concern of the college age adolescent, we have found that this conceptualization is inadequate for understanding the concerns of the younger adolescents. It appears that young adolescents must resolve questions about their relationship to peer groups before they can fully resolve questions about their relationship to their family and to themselves. It seems to us quite critical that the young adolescent develop the sense of group identity as a prelude to a sense of personal identity.[5]

**Being "Invited" Is Crucial**
Ministerial efforts with Quicksilvers need to be attentive to this psychosocial concern. Young people do not automatically claim membership in a group. They have a need to identify with and belong to a group, but they are reticent about making the initial moves toward membership. Part of our empowerment for this stage includes awareness of the value of continuous personal invitations as we attempt to include Quicksilvers in our programming.

A personal invitation is one way we can subtly inform young people that we regard them as persons of value. We let them know through our invitation that they are welcome and needed. Our group can become their group. Our invitation is our way of informing them that *we* have *chosen* them. Our choice builds their self-esteem and their response to join us reinforces their positive regard of their self-worth.

Let's return for a minute to our friend Jeff. He is at a critical moment in his personality development and its accrued virtues. Rejection and neglect have been his major experiences in life. He has no reason to trust his environment or his significant others.

Amazingly enough, he has thus far survived and shows both initiative and competence in his attempts to serve as his own caregiver. Jeff is at a crucial crossroad in his life. He needs a support system, a group with whom to identify, and he needs to know he is worthy of our care. He represents a growing minority among the young people we serve, those who are marginalized. They are the potential heartbreaks of youth ministry because they are youth-at-risk and could easily slip out of life.

Once people like Jeff enter our ministry, we must respond as their advocates. They have had life experiences that hamper their ability to resolve life's stages (as described by Erikson) on their own.

What are some of the practical questions Jeff's advocate would need to investigate? Would Jeff's teachers and boss treat him differently if they knew his circumstances? Could the school counselor help Jeff get tutoring and/or study help at school? Is Jeff's future brother-in-law really a "jerk" or is it that he doesn't realize the hardships Jeff is enduring? Are there people in the parish that could help with Jeff's employment by giving Jeff rides to work on rainy days, using Jeff for their yard work, or offering some other kind of employment? Is there someone in the parish who would act as Jeff's "big brother" or surrogate family?

People in parishes are usually willing to help those who are marginalized if they are empowered to know what can be done. It is our responsibility as ministers to stay aware of the other people in the parish who can be a part of our ministry to these forgotten youth.

We cannot allow the Jeffs in our lives to be lost, if at all possible. They are God's children and we are called to find ways to "recycle" their experiences of trust and autonomy so that they recognize their worth. It is through new experiences of trust, confidence, and love that they will develop the ego strength necessary to fulfill their potential as adults.

## Re-Experiencing Earlier Tasks

In *Becoming the Way We Are*[6] Pam Levin identifies an interesting phenomenon called "recycling." Earlier tasks of development are re-experienced and re-lived as a person progresses through a new stage of development. Levin says that this phenomenon occurs all through life, but is easily recognized in adolescence.

Let us investigate recycling, looking first at 13 year olds who relive infancy. At 13 we begin a new birth. Just like an infant, we eat all the time; want to be the center of attention and have high stroking needs. We have a shortened attention span and constantly try to get attention through loud behavior. (This worked when we were infants!) We have difficulty making simple decisions: what to wear, how to do simple household tasks, completing homework, etc., but we want assistance only if we request it, not if an adult suggests it! The added agenda that separates us from infancy is that now we have a heightened awareness of sexuality and we spend a lot of time thinking about the opposite sex.

At 14 we resemble a two year old in temperament. We are stubborn, negative, compliant or rebellious (depending on our mood), and messy. We frequently forget normal everyday tasks, like turning off the faucet of an overflowing bathtub! We are sometimes accused of being stupid by our caregivers and often that is exactly what we are convinced we are. We test controls constantly and are often very unpleasant to live with!

At 15 we relive our third year of life. We argue and hassle to be allowed to do anything we choose to do. We usually try to figure out how to do things differently than the way other people tell us to do them. Our sexual energies are now a constant part of who we are, and these energies add to mood swings and irritability.

What's going on here? Life with these young people sounds so negative. In my dealings with adolescents and their families over the past decade, I have watched parents struggle with this time in their child's life. The negative behavior is problematic but understandable. The young are in a very important time of life. They are preparing for a "friendly divorce from their guardians."[7] They need to emerge as separate, complete beings with a distinct identity from that of their parents. Parents usually remember their own struggles as adolescents, but wrestle with the necessity of "letting go" and allowing their child to become a distinct entity.

I believe that the hardest part of this time of development for young adolescents is that they fear they will never separate from their parents or that they will be forced to separate from their parents before they're ready! Sound confusing? The behavior we see is a clear indication that it *is* confusing. The young person thinks, "If I am obnoxious enough, they will leave me alone, and it will be easier to separate. But if I am too obnoxious, they may ask me to leave before I'm ready!"

This time of life is so difficult for parents because their children often send opposing signals. "Treat me like a child when I need to be like a child," the young seem to say. "Pay my way into activities, protect me from authorities, etc., but treat me like an adult when I want to do something I want to do!" It's no wonder that parents dread this time of parenting and need as much affirmation as their children.

In many ways, recycling can give us a chance to rework the developmental tasks whose resolution were hindered by life crises. It provides all of us and especially our youth-at-risk with the opportunity to reconstruct and rework issues that could affect our later lives. Recycling is the "second chance" and the "starting over" that many of us dream about, but fail to realize is possible! Parents can be helped to regard this time as less negative when they are informed of the value of recycling, not only for their young, but for themselves as well.

As we attempt to minister to the total person, we need to consider activities and life experiences that affirm a young person's involvement in the recycling process. Parents can be affirmed as they learn to recognize characteristics that indicate their youngsters are growing up!

## Moral and Faith Development
To conclude our discussion of development, let's turn to three

theorists: Lawrence Kohlberg, Carol Gilligan, and James Fowler.[8] Their combined works give us a sketch of typical characteristics of the faith journey of Quicksilvers.

Young adolescents hunger for acceptance and approval of others. Conformity is highly valued and they purposely design their personal actions so that significant others notice and affirm them. They judge the behavior of others by its intention. "What did you mean by what you did?" is a key question in their judgment of behavior.

Girls in this stage of development have a strong bias for empathy. They feel what others feel. They operate out of their understanding of the interconnectedness of relationships and generally make decisions which include consideration for all persons involved. Boys, on the other hand, make decisions based on what the majority says is right. Both boys and girls behave according to what they perceive to be the "nice" thing to do.

For some, the basis for their moral reasoning is formed by the authority and laws of society. They display a moral stance characterized by an internalization of the social order. They will defend, argue for, and operate out of the "status quo" that society says is the norm.

A prominent characteristic of young people this age is the complexity of their relationships. Their world is now extended far beyond family. They now are involved in many arenas of life and relationships: family, school, peers, leisure, friendships, church, etc. Faith is the activity that the young person uses to make meaning out of this complex world. They gain a coherent and meaningful synthesis of the influx of differing attitudes, values and beliefs by following the authority of those "in charge," be they significant adults or peers. It depends on who they are with at the moment, as to who they deem the "authority."

Young people at this stage of development tend to "compartmentalize." They act one way with peers and another way at home. This compartmentalization of behavior is a result of the complexity of their relationships and the differing views of all the people who inhabit their day-to-day world.

A significant aspect at this stage is the role of symbols.

The individual understands metaphors and the double entendre and is preparing to allow symbols to affect him or her at a variety of levels simultaneously. The symbol and the symbolized are correlated. Typical images of God are based on "personal" qualities of the diety, i.e., friend, comforter, guide, etc."[9]

Symbols that now possess a distinct personal quality allow the young person to relate to a "personal" God, as illustrated by the following prayer.

I know God hears me. I pray every night and I can feel God's forgiveness and love for me. I have prayed for things that God has granted. I know that I did not deserve for these things to happen. They happened because God heard me and cares for my needs. —Simone, age 14

**A Crucial Turning Point**
Early adolescents operating out of characteristics described above have journeyed to a crucial point of religious development. They now have a capacity for understanding religious language as symbolic rather than literal. The young person now has developed the capacity to understand that the interrelationship between God and us and other people is dialogical. They see that our connectedness to God is not one-sided. It is truly a relationship.

Quicksilvers are ripe and eager for encounters with the person of Jesus. They genuinely hunger for a meaningful relationship with God. Expressions of faith that are merely cultural and lack the power of a deep conviction do not attract them. They need and want a God who makes a difference and a religion that can affect the lives of its followers at their deepest level. Young people are attracted to adults who have responded to such demands and who sincerely believe they have found something worthwhile to share. Genuine faith, consistent honesty and mature commitment by respected elders gives them strength through a vision of what they can someday be.

Understanding the developmental characteristics normal to young adolescents empowers the adults who work with them to respect and affirm each individual as a unique reflection of God. Quicksilvers can be wonderful reminders that life is full of joy and an adventure to be experienced with openness and delight! Their boundless energy and eagerness to belong are invaluable assets for our attempts to include partnership as an important component of our ministry "with" the young adolescent.

Their honesty is their greatest gift to our ministry. They will love us and thank us for letting them be the "living fluidity" whose restlessness brings us all to a new understanding of our God! The following poem sums up a Quicksilver's honest feelings about this stage of life.

>
> Where
> Can I meet
> This God
> Of Whom
> You preach?
> You
> Say that I can encounter
> This Love-Force
> In the Word,
> In the Sacraments.
> But
> I have sat
> In silent pews
> And "Heard" this Word.
> But
> I have marched
> Through empty rituals

And have been sacramented
And
I have yet to recognize
This love
This joy
This Ultimate
In those untouchable actions.
You
Say that I can also encounter
This Love-Force
In others.
So I come
Answering your invitation
To look deeper.
And
I timidly open
Myself…
Trusting,
Risking,
Searching,
And I find "me"
And I find "you"
And I find "God"
Thank you!

—Shannon, age 15

## Notes

1. Joan Scheff Lipsitz, "Adolescent Development: Myths and Realities" *Early Adolescent Series* (Carrboro, N.C.: Center for Early Adolescence, University of North Carolina at Chapel Hill, 1982), p. 1.

2. John S. Darcy, *Adolescents Today* (Glenview, Ill.: Scott, Foresman & Co., 1982), p. 103.

3. Between 1982 and the present, I have interviewed over 100 early adolescents in the southwestern region of the United States. These young people represented all racial groups and were either active in their parish/diocesan youth programs or attended a Catholic high school. The only criteria was that they were "not yet 16." Sometimes the interviews were conducted face to face. Sometimes they were conducted through an anonymous written survey and sometimes they were conducted through a question/answer letter exchange.

4. The above information is compiled from: Erik Erikson, *Childhood and Society*, second ed. (New York: W.W. Norton, 1963), Chapter 7.

5. Barbara M. and Philip R. Newman, *Development Through Life: A Psychosocial Approach*, rev. ed. (Homewood, Ill.: Dorey Press, 1979), p. 268.

6. This section is drawn from Pam Levin, *Becoming the Way We Are* (Berkeley, Cal.: Transactional Publications, 1974), pp. 50-52.

7. Ibid. p. 51.

8. This section is a composite taken from the following:
Ronald Duska, Mariellen Whelan, *Moral Development* (New York: Paulist Press, 1975), p. 46.
Carol Gilligan, *In a Different Voice* (Cambridge, Mass.: Harvard University Press, 1982), p. 8.
James Fowler, "Stages in Faith: The Structural Developmental Approach," *Values and Moral Development*, Thomas C. Hennessey, ed. (New York: Paulist Press, 1976), p. 184.

9. James Fowler and Sam Keene, *Life Maps: Conversations on the Journey of Faith*, Jerome Berryman, ed. (Waco, Tex.: Word Books, 1978), p. 64.

Chapter 2

*How Should We Minister with Quicksilvers?*

# Foundational Elements for Ministry

Young adolescents experience loneliness, alienation, and powerlessness in many areas of their lives. The emptiness these feelings produce cries out for a connection with a compassionate community rooted in the belief that each individual has worth and dignity. When young people engage in a genuine relationship with God they learn that they are never alone and that they truly belong. The church then becomes a healing environment, offering the acceptance and the support that challenge the death-dealing systems in our society.

I have often heard it said that a society's greatest resource is its young. That resource, I believe, is threatened today by consumerism, substance abuse, and premature sexual activity. Countering such social dangers is one of the more monumental tasks the church faces today. Never before have our values been challenged as openly as they are in today's society. The young have become targets in a destructive cycle that values instant gratification, self-indulgence and escapism.

Programming to combat these problems is presently concentrated on the high school years which, in many instances, is too late. The "forgotten age group," the 10 to 16 year olds, must become the focal point of our ministerial efforts. These Quicksilvers need to feel valued because of who they are, not because of what they look like, what they wear, or how much money is in their pockets.

Young people in this age group need skills for relating to others in non-genital ways. Similarly, they must learn that alcohol consumption is not a rite of passage but a pathway to self-destruction. Finally, they need opportunities to experience simple, joyful ways to spend their leisure time.

In my work with young people, I see they want answers for their basic questions—what gives life meaning, and how does one discover if one is successful? Unfortunately, Madison Avenue has invested millions of dollars proposing answers to these questions and has confused the abilities of the young to discern reality from fantasy and necessities from luxuries. This confusion leads young adolescents to heights of restless dissatisfaction with self, possessions, and lifestyle.

**A Story about John, age 16**
When I was 14, I felt that in order to be popular, I had to have Calvin Klein jeans, Reebok sneakers, and a specific hair style. I made up stories about my parents, saying they belonged to the country club and drove an Alfa Romeo.

But actually my mom worked as a teacher and my dad did not live with us. In a way that made my lies easier. I made up this incredible story about my dad's big city job. I said he flew all around the world, drove a Porsche, and lived in a condo overlooking a lake.

I started stealing to get money for the things I wanted. I told everyone my dad sent me money whenever I needed it. At first, I stole from my mom, but when she got suspicious I found an easier, larger source.

My friends left money all over their rooms. I could usually pick up ten to twenty dollars every time I visited someone. Once I stole from a friend's mother's purse. She had five $100 bills in her wallet. I was tempted to take all of them, but I figured she wouldn't miss one bill and might just think the bank had made a mistake. I was right. No one ever mentioned missing money.

This continued for about a year. I always had $20 in my wallet and sometimes I treated the whole group to pizza. Do you know what the worst part was? I was very, very popular! I began to live in fear that I would get caught or that the other kids would find out that my dad never called and that he drove a truck in Tulsa. I didn't like my life and I began to hate myself. I was so glad when my mom and I moved. That probably saved me from getting into something worse.

Where was the gospel in John's life? He was responding to the values of a consumer society that says more and more expensive is better. The dishonesty and self-hatred that he experienced will continue to permeate his life unless he is presented with alternatives. The church with its mission to share the good news, can offer people like John reconciliation and redemption, and we who are in youth ministry should be representatives of this message.

Young adolescents need us to help them strengthen egos and enhance the skills necessary to reverse the influence of consumerism. Our ministry can enable them to recognize the hopes and future promised by Jesus in the gospels.

## We Start by Inviting

One cold December morning I sat at my desk opening cards from friends and parishioners when I came upon one with no return address. The handwriting looked familiar and curiosity heightened my holiday joy and fun-filled mood! Opening it, I found it was from one of those rare young people who recognizes the humanness of adults and our need for expressions of thanks and encouragement. Her letter said:

I remember seventh grade and our first youth group activity. One of the things you said to us was that in this youth group we didn't have to worry about being anything other than who we are. We didn't have to wear masks and hide our true selves. We were welcome to just come with no pressures to try to "fit in." We were part of this group with no effort of our own.

When the older kids took us one-on-one, I really felt I counted! After that experience, I understood more and more why an accepting attitude was so important to me. I could just "be"—I loved the church at that moment for the first time in my life! I will always treasure the fact that I can toss off my masks and just be free to enjoy being who I am as church and as part of a youth group. Thank you.

Love, Jennifer

Invitation and a comfortable atmosphere of acceptance are key elements in our ministry to young adolescents. The fragility of their sense of self and the societal pressures they meet in their everyday lives make our ministerial efforts with them more important than they have ever been before.

But our ministry with the young must be grounded in an understanding of the mission and ministry of the whole church. We are a community of people who espouse a belief in the salvific action of God through the life of Jesus Christ. We also believe that our own works and lives are permeated by the actions of the Holy Spirit. The church is that environment in which young people meet the person of Jesus and come to recognize the work of the Holy Spirit in their own lives. We invite them into this environment for the same three reasons we invite anyone: "to proclaim the good news of salvation to all humankind; to offer ourselves as a group of people transformed by the Spirit into a community of faith, hope and love; and to bring God's justice and love to others through service in the church's individual, social and political dimensions."[1]

Ministry is the "ways and means" of fulfilling this mission. Each member of the church community has a call to share in the responsibility of ministering to others. Responding to our unique God-given gifts, each of us must identify that portion of the mission that best utilizes our talents. Using Jesus as a model, we discover the importance of God in our lives as we share the faith journeys of others.

Imitating Jesus, we are called to "put aside" our own needs to respond to the needs of others. It is this sacrifice that frees others to recognize God's unique presence in their lives and offers them opportunities to share themselves.

> Because ministry involves the giving of self in relationship to another, the church's youth ministry must be founded in the radical commitment to lay down one's life in service to the young people whose lives are touched. The primacy of this loving gift of self ensures fidelity to the ministry of Jesus and guides the work of youth ministry in fulfilling the church's three-fold mission of Word, Community and Service.[2]

## The Importance of Principles

In the winter of 1986, I was invited by my diocesan Youth Director to represent the Archdiocese of Oklahoma City on the National Federation for Catholic Youth Ministry's Committee on Adolescent Catechesis. Since that time I have become a strong advocate for the resourcing and networking that originates with the Federation's working committees.

I have always sensed a need to express some grounding principles for my own ministry with adolescents. As I travel around the country doing workshops and planning programs for parish youth ministry, I have discovered that many people are unaware that in 1976 the United States Catholic Conference produced a position paper called *A Vision of Youth Ministry*. This work has provided the foundational grounding for youth ministry in most

Roman Catholic settings for the past two decades. It says above all that "youth ministry is *to, with, by,* and *for* youth."³

These four dimensions identify components for effective youth ministry. But what does this string of prepositions mean? In my work with young people I have noticed a pattern that evolves when young people are affirmed and invited to take part in their own programming. This pattern is like the ripple effect when a pebble is tossed into a pool of water. When the young are ministered to, they feel a need to minister. When they minister, a mutuality is established between themselves and the adults involved. When the adults begin to see the young as co-workers for bringing about the reign of God, the adults find themselves speaking out more and more for youth concerns.

When we program "to" youth, we are utilizing the most common and traditional element of youth ministry. We, the adults, design activities such as scouts, catechetical or Sunday school programs, sports, etc., for youth who are the "subjects" of the programs. Leadership, planning, and training are almost always characterized by an "adults only" mentality. For many years all of our ministerial efforts with young people fell into this category. Commonly known under the umbrella term "CYO," this model is still prevalent in many parts of the country today. It's an important element of youth ministry, but it is no longer enough. This dimension alone does not give young people sufficient grounding to internalize the values and mandates of the gospel.

Ministry that is "with" youth is inclusive in all ways. There is mutuality and shared responsibility when adults and youth work and minister side-by-side. This component is most effective when the youth involved are truly regarded as equals and partners in the process. Activities such as leadership teams, retreat teams, community service, fund-raising, etc. are examples of this dimension.

Youth ministry "by" youth is the dimension least incorporated in most programs. It involves a "letting go" by adults and includes activities designed and carried out by young people themselves.

It is often a subtle and unorganized attempt by the young to "test their wings." Follow through skills are often lacking and mistakes are made. A program that deletes this dimension, however, denies the basic premise of Christianity that all members of the community are gifted and called to share their unique gifts. Activities such as peer drug counseling, support groups, liturgical planning teams, etc. are a few examples. This dimension needs a creative consideration of how to empower young people to minister to each other and to the wider community.

**One of the Most Crucial**
Youth ministry "for" youth is one of the most crucial in today's society. The young often have no voice in many of the decisions that impact their lives. They are exploited by the media and often misunderstood by the general public. Adults who take youth seriously often find themselves defending youth, interpreting their behavior and advocating their rights and concerns to others.

> The adult involved in youth ministry has special access to the views of youth, and ordinarily has a degree of credibility, influence and resources unavailable to young people. This places a responsibility on the adult to speak for youth and to sensitize and motivate other adults where youth needs are concerned.[4]

Each dimension is distinct and important to the development of a *total* youth ministry. Organizations such as Youth Specialties, Group, Center for Youth Ministry Development, and NFCYM spend time and resources developing programs and publications and arranging public gatherings to enhance our efforts to incorporate all these dimensions into our local planning. Networking at conferences, diocesan gatherings and workshops could become a creative force that enriches all aspects of these dimensions for our future ministerial efforts among young adolescents. And all are appropriate for even the youngest adolescent. The personal dignity and integrity of their unique stage of life needs to be honored and affirmed. Adults need to remember that these young people are also touched by God and empowered by the Spirit to respond to the life and teachings of Jesus.

The *Vision* document identifies two goals that help us see the multi-dimensional aspect of youth ministry more clearly. These are: 1) fostering the total personal and spiritual growth of each young person; 2) drawing young people to responsible participation in the life, mission and work of the faith community.[5] I would add a third goal for youth ministry with Quicksilvers in mind: 3) providing a "safe" environment of unconditional acceptance of each young person involved.

These goals encourage us to invite, accept and empower young people to become all they are created to be: viable members of the Christian community—the young church of today!

Six principles of effective youth ministry devised by the NFCYM "give youth ministry character and underlie its effectiveness."[6] These principles could serve as grounding principles for all ministry. When applied specifically to youth, they help to flesh out the importance of an intentional activity of the church toward its young.

**1. Youth is a unique time of personal development.** An important task of anyone who deals with adolescents, particularly those in ministry, is to help the young "celebrate their time." This is not a time of life one simply waits out. It is a vitally important stage of life. Parents need to be supported and their efforts to deal with their children affirmed so that they can cope with this transitional stage of development and enjoy and celebrate the uniqueness of their child's life journey.

**2. Youth ministry is concerned with the total person.** Being Christian doesn't involve just our religious times; it involves all of our being and is a full-time endeavor. The total person needs nurturing and affirmation in his or her social, cultural, educational, and spiritual realms.

3. **Youth ministry is rooted in relationships.** Relationships that invite us to honor ourselves and others are the framework for our growing relationships with God. It is primarily in our interactions with others that we learn to accept or negate our "self." Relating is the key activity of adolescents. Affirming relationships call the young beyond themselves and provide the support for their maturing in faith.

4. **Youth ministry is a call to community.** Youth Ministry does not survive in one-on-one relationships. Cultic groupings around a particular person are not real ministry. It is in inclusive community that young people will find reciprocity. In community they reach out to others and experience a response as an affirmation. And when others reach out to them, they find themselves willing to respond. It is only within community that they will truly experience the power of the "good news" that we are called to serve others.

5. **Youth ministry proceeds as an affirmation of gifts.** By affirming the unique gifts and talents of the young people to whom we minister, we nurture their abilities and invite them to develop their full potential, giving birth to positive experiences of self-esteem.

6. **True ministry duplicates itself.** If we genuinely model our ministry after Jesus, we will "let go" and send our young people out to serve others. Standing aside, we witness the true treasure of ministry; those to whom we minister become ministers to others.

These principles provide the foundation for what we are about—encouraging the young church of today to become a powerful element in the church of tomorrow.

The foundational structure shaped by all the dimensions, goals, principles and components developed by NFCYM give us a solid grounding for our service to young adolescents. Ministry is first of all a response, a response to the needs of the community, a response to the needs of the church. Adolescence is the time of searching and claiming. These foundational elements honor adolescent needs and challenge young people to look beyond the present so that they are sponsored on this important step in their faith journey. It is within this framework that the young people to whom we minister discover their own role in the mission of the church.

### A Story about Angela, age 13

When I first met Angela, I was immediately drawn to her friendliness and eagerness to be a part of our youth program. She was mature for her age, full of energy, highly regarded by her peers and had supportive parents. She wanted to do everything! She was the first to sign up for every event we advertised. She campaigned vigorously for the seventh-grade position on our Youth Council and was soon sharing creative ideas about how the youth group could be more involved in the community. Almost before the rest of the kids noticed, she had us signed up to help restore a Habitat for Humanity house. She also managed to recruit five new seventh graders into the program.

Angela is the dream child of every youth minister. She is the kind of person who comes along only once every few years. The six years that she will be in the program will be an innovative time. She is already involving her peers and shows true promise as a leader in peer ministry. She is socially aware and will provide challenges for all of us as we respond to the mission of the church and reach out to others. With Angela, the foundational goals and components of effective youth ministry are not just an ideal, they are an exciting possibility!

## Notes

1. Richard P. McBrien, *Church: The Continuing Quest* (New Jersey: Newman Press, 1970), p. 73.

2. Department of Education for the United States Catholic Conference, *A Vision of Youth Ministry* (Washington, D.C., 1986), p. 4.

3. Ibid., p. 6.

4. Ibid., p. 7.

5. Ibid.

6. Ibid., p. 8.

Chapter 3

*What Stresses and Pressures Are on Quicksilvers?*

# Self, Family, Friends, School, Media

Lindy and Lacy are sisters who live apart. At 14, Lindy lives with their father and Lacy, who is 13, lives with their mother. Until recently, the girls never questioned this living arrangement. They haven't lived together since their parents divorced eight years ago. They hardly know each other and they spend very little time together. Recently their mother changed jobs. She and Lacy moved, and Lacy entered the same school that Lindy attends.

The sisters look remarkably alike and many people mistake them for twins. Their peers have begun to ask embarrassing questions about their family situation and both girls are uncomfortable with their notoriety. Lindy particularly resents that their mother did not consult her about Lacy's school transfer. She is running for class president and she is afraid that her "weird family set-up" will hurt her chances.

"Everyone stares at me now when I walk down the halls. Even the teachers! I know they are wondering about my family and I know they are not sure if I am me or if I am Lacy. The other day the cutest boy in eighth grade phoned me. I was so excited until he called me Lacy! I have never been so embarrassed in my life! I just know all my friends will find out about this and I will be the butt of jokes in the lunch room. I know everyone looks at me and thinks I'm some kind of a weirdo!"

Lindy displays a characteristic common to Quicksilvers—extreme self-consciousness. Dr. David Elkind in *All Grown Up and No Place to Go* names this behavior "imaginary audience."

> Because teenagers are caught up with the transformations they are undergoing: in their bodies, in their facial structure, in their feelings and emotions, and in their thinking powers, they become self-centered about the same thing they are concerned with, namely themselves. Teenagers feel they are always on stage and that everyone around them is as aware of and as concerned about their appearance and behavior as they themselves are. They stubbornly believe they are the focus of everyone's abiding attention and concern. Hence they are very self-conscious and often go to extreme lengths to avoid what they are convinced will be mortifying experiences.[1]

**Everyone Is Looking**
Lindy is positive she is now the object of negative attention at school. She centers on her "self" as the focus of everyone's attention. This behavioral stance seems to be reinforced by peers who continually encourage self-consciousness by blatantly noticing every out-of-the-ordinary life occurrence, every out-of-place hair, every new facial blemish, and even the "wrong" name brand of clothes. As a result, Quicksilvers appear to be self-centered and are often the target of negative criticism from adults. Those adults who make the mistake of publicly criticizing or ridiculing these young people risk a complete loss of credibility with them. Young adolescents are extremely vulnerable to criticism of any kind and generally lack the ego-strength to recognize

criticism as constructive. Significant adults should be aware of this over-sensitivity to public exposure and be sensitive that the criticism they offer is more volatile than they think.

Another indicator of "imaginary audience-at-work" is what I call "mirror time." Young adolescents spend an incredible amount of their day in front of mirrors. This is not motivated by vanity but its opposite. Self-consciousness and the fear of imperfection draw them to the mirror. Thus a vicious cycle is set in motion as the young person "imagines" the worst and the imperfect reflection observed in the mirror confirms negative regard of self.

An important element of our ministerial efforts with adolescents is to intentionally contradict those experiences that affirm their self dislike. Our endeavors to enhance their self-like should include occasions in which we sponsor genuine friendships between young people. When people are recognized and valued for who they are, and not for what they look like or what they wear or for their life circumstances, they begin to value themselves. Adolescents can learn that perfection is often an ideal determined by imperfect others. Positive relationships with others can help them to recognize that all people are at times insecure and self-conscious, and that no one is perfect.

Elkind identifies another phenomenon common to this age group which he calls "personal fable." "Perhaps because teenagers are so convinced that people are observing and thinking about them, they get an inflated opinion of their own importance. They begin to feel they are special and unique."[2]

The negative side to this stance is that the young person feels that "nothing bad will ever happen to me or to those I love." A sense of invincibility permeates the typical adolescent's behavior, sometimes manifested by high speed driving, drinking while driving, unprotected sexual activity, and other dangerous behaviors. The young person seems to lose all rationality and to have no regard for consequences. Reminders of the uniqueness of all people and reminders that others have a right to expect responsible behavior can help young adolescents tread cautiously while holding on to their fable and enjoying the sense of invulnerability it affords.

"Imaginary audience" and "personal fable" are not characteristics of adolescent behavior only. All through life we are dissatisfied with our imperfections and experience moments of self-consciousness and insecurity. We tolerate such moments because as adults we can cope with negative feelings when we have gained the wisdom that accompanies a strong sense of self. Without some sense of personal fable we would never take risks or try things that are new and challenging. Hope is born alongside personal fable and it is hope that empowers us to trust in God. These two kinds of thinking, while at times negative in adolescence, stay with us into adulthood and help us to develop trust in ourselves as capable and hope-filled people.

## Children of Divorce

Let's look at another factor affecting Lindy and Lacy. They are children of divorce, an element of their story that has become more common among adolescents in the last 25 years.

Of all the changes in American society in recent years, those affecting the structure of the family are among the most extensive. It is estimated that one-fifth of all children in the United States live in a single parent household and that 63 percent of all women work outside the home. The traditional two-parent family is under pressure and losing its dominance in American society. According to a recent study by *Newsweek* magazine only about 26 percent of the households in this country are two-parent households.[3]

In 1850, the average size of the American household was eight. Today the average household size is 2.3 people, and this figure is continually dropping.[4]

Add to these changes the fact that the average American family moves every five years, and we find many challenges that will shape the future of our ministry with young adolescents.

Each of the societal factors mentioned above influences youth differently. High mobility tends to isolate the nuclear family from its roots. Who functions as the nurturer and socializer of the young when women's roles change and so many work outside of the home? Who, with mothers gone and fewer siblings, do Quicksilvers model themselves after? Young people are at a greater risk than ever before for stress-related maladies that often accompany loneliness and feelings of alienation. Young adolescents make up the largest population of latch-key or unsupervised children during the hours between 3:00 and 7:00 P.M. Too old for after-school babysitters, they are too young for after-school jobs.

One of the key services we can offer Quicksilvers is an after-school program. In the parish where I serve as youth minister we schedule three afternoons a week as "drop-in" time. The youth help each other with homework, play games, and have an opportunity to be with other young people during the long afternoons while their parents are working. People in youth ministry must deal with these crucial issues. Any effort to minister to young people must consider the family context.

The good news is that when parents communicate clearly and consistently and do not lay their own emotional baggage on their children, their marital state makes no difference to their effectiveness as parents. Parents hunger for and have a genuine need for support in their attempts to effectively parent adolescents. Programs that inform them of the normalcy of their child's developmental characteristics, enhance communication skills between parent and child, and empower parents to openly discuss sexuality and other difficult issues, build parent self-esteem.

**Why Friends Are Important**
Quicksilvers love to interact with one another. Young adolescents tend to search out relationships that are affirming. Within the framework of friendship, they often test ideas and values, explore multitudes of new thoughts, and dare to risk rejection by

sharing dreams. There is no better place for youth to learn the skills of interpersonal relationships than among equals. Learning to relate by relating in an accepting environment provides a structure for Quicksilvers to move from a family-centered world to another-centered way of life. Friends provide the means to laugh with someone, to contemplate life's meaning, to play, and to experience love and loyalty with someone who is not a family member. Friends, second only to parents, become the strongest influence on a maturing adolescent's search for identity. They provide opportunities for young adolescents to become connected to a "group" that is outside the home. Friends help friends solve problems, especially when one or the other comes from a dysfunctional or troubled family.

A quick observation: Go to any mall in this country on a weekend afternoon or evening and sit quietly in an isolated corner. In a very short time you will observe young adolescents in "relationship." Invariably, they travel in same-gender packs. They are in constant motion and conversation, and they roam the mall in search of adventure. Malls are fast becoming the "street corners" of this age. This space becomes the gathering place for conversations and ritualized behaviors. It is an important part of a Quicksilver's social life. Everything is at hand: food, entertainment, peers, and the latest fashions. One does not have to have a driver's license to enjoy a bit of freedom. To be dropped off at the mall, unaccompanied by adults, is a mini-rite of passage for 11 to 13 year olds.

At times, the stress Quicksilvers experience as a result of establishing and maintaining friendships is compounded by the conflicts they face when the values of their peers clash with the values of significant adults, especially parents.

Peer pressure is an expected and dreaded part of growing up for a teenager in today's society. There are mixed reactions on the subject of stress and pressure among experts on adolescence, and there is little empirical data to substantiate that peer pressure can and does exert negative control over a young person's life. Personal conversations with youth and their parents, however, definitely point to a significant amount of stress. By the time they reach junior high, young people have heard all the myths and look forward to peer relationships with some fear and trepidation. And at some time during adolescence most youngsters will experience at least one incident where they will let peer pressure influence them to engage in negative behavior.

Increasing evidence suggests that self-esteem and open communication with parents produce the kind of decisiveness that enables a young person to combat negative peer pressure. In the May 1991 issue of *Reader's Digest*, Kathleen McCoy suggests how parents can help their children deal with negative peer pressure.

> While many parents feel powerless to make a difference, experts say they are actually in the best position to help their kids resist troublesome urgings from peers.[5]

She suggests strategies for parents, including daily listening to their child's concerns, explaining possible outcomes of their child's decisions in troublesome situations, role-playing, intentional bolstering of their child's sense of self, and continual expressions of unconditional love.

**Parents Need Support**
"The years you spend parenting an adolescent are perhaps among the most difficult times you'll have as a parent," I recently stated to a group of 50 adults who were attending classes designed for parents of teenagers. "The stresses and pressures your child faces during this period of life are duplicative, that is, they often become your stresses and pressures, too!" This information was affirmed by 50 nodding heads. When I asked these adults what their greatest fear about their child's adolescence was, the overwhelming response was the fear that their children would buckle under negative peer pressure.

The evening continued with people sharing their experiences

of helping their children cope with pressure from peers. We all listened with amazement at a story from Jerry. He and his wife, Janice, are regarded as among the most successful parents of adolescents in the parish. They have four children ages 19, 17, 16, and 13. In any conversation regarding who is considered a "model family" in the community, their names surface. Jerry and Janice communicate well with their children and often ask their childrens' opinions on a variety of subjects. Their children are generally well-liked by their peers and are often selected for leadership roles in school and at church youth activities.

Here was Jerry's story.

Todd returned home from an afternoon at the mall where he was to have met two friends to go to a movie. He was very quiet at dinner and we could tell that something was bothering him. After dinner, he went alone to his room where I found him stretched out on his bed staring at the ceiling. When I asked him what was wrong, he turned to me with tears in his eyes and said, "You're going to hate me, Dad. I have done something terrible." I held my breath for a moment and told him that there was absolutely nothing he could ever do that would cause me to hate him, and that he would feel better if he told me about it.

Todd recounted his afternoon. He and his friends had not attended a movie. Instead they had decided to "goof off" by checking out several of the new stores in the mall. One of the youngsters dared the others to shoplift items from a sporting goods store. The challenge was to see who could steal the largest item. Todd said that at first he had refused to take part, but the others made fun of him, so he finally agreed. Todd hung his head for a moment and finally continued his account.

He told me he had won the challenge by stealing a basketball that was still in its box. "The others thought I was really cool, Dad, but I knew I wasn't. We sat outside the mall and counted our loot and we figured we had stolen about $100 worth of stuff. I was feeling bad enough when Larry saw some other kids we knew from school and started bragging to them about what we had done. He even convinced them to try to see if anyone could beat me! That's when I yelled, 'no,' grabbed all the stuff, went back into the store and put it back on the shelves. Then I came home. I feel like a jerk, Dad. I can't believe I let them talk me into it.

Jerry went on to share that he and Janice both had separate conversations with Todd about how they were proud of the way he resolved the situation. They discussed his feelings when he discovered his inability to resist in this situation. They both assured him that they loved him and knew he was disappointed in himself, but there was no reason to dwell on this incident, but to learn from his mistake and to face up to his friends in the future.

Parents who genuinely like their children and exert efforts to understand their struggles decrease their childrens' vulnerability to negative pressures.

This issue again illustrates an important area where we in ministry can empower the parents of the young people we serve. By recognizing and affirming their attempts to have a positive influence on their children, we can help to strengthen parenting skills that build self-esteem, not only in their children but in themselves as well.

We also must use every opportunity to assert our own influence on Quicksilvers' struggles to face up to their peers. As youth ministers, we often have opportunities that many parents don't, opportunities to sponsor friendships between young people, but also opportunities to challenge negative influences young people exert on one another.

A final word on friends: This area is perhaps the most crucial in our ministry to Quicksilvers. To be 13 and without a friend can be one of the most devastating experiences in life.

**A Story about Terry, age 13**
One Sunday evening, I answered my phone with the typical

hesitancy of every tired person who yearns for quiet at the end of the longest day of the week. It was Terry, one of the parish's marginal youths, an eighth grader who infrequently attended religion classes and youth group but who had recently attended a 24-hour overnight retreat. He wanted to talk to me, and as usual with adolescents, that request meant "right now, please!"

I arranged to meet Terry for a country drive, my normal one-on-one environment for counseling adolescents, a technique that insures undivided quality time with only the beauty of Oklahoma wheat fields as distraction.

In the car Terry's eyes welled with tears as he described the current crisis that affirmed his self-hatred. I listened and considered again the importance of presence in ministry to this neglected age group. Terry's quest is painful, but appropriate. He called me because he felt an overwhelming sense of loneliness. He felt left out and didn't know "where he belonged." He wasn't getting along with his parents; he felt ignored and discounted at school; he didn't fit in with the kids at church, and he was without a best friend.

Terry desperately needed to belong. He was missing out on the joy of life as he struggled to identify where he fit. His self-esteem was shaky and he was unlikely to risk rejection in order to find "his" group. He desperately needed a friend. Recognition of his vulnerability and a gentle affirmation of him as a worthwhile and important human being were the focus of my first few meetings with him.[6]

Eventually I invited other young people to join us on our country drives. I became more and more of an observer as the young people gained trust in each other and began to engage in conversation and playful banter. A few weeks later, Terry and several other country-riders formed a work team to help me prepare the parish building and grounds for parish gatherings. Several times Terry and a few others accompanied me to our local soup kitchen where we helped the staff empty trash, clean tables, and do other odd jobs. Talking and laughing with others while riding in the country, moving potted plants in church, weeding a flower bed, and feeding the poor, Terry soon was a member of a group. Two months after that initial phone call, Terry had a best friend and no longer depended on my initiatives to assure him that he was a worthwhile human person.

Opportunities for friendship are there for young people and one of our more important roles as ministers may very well be to provide them with experiences that empower them to risk.

### A Story about Danny, age 12

Danny has just completed his second week of seventh grade and also has just experienced the most traumatic events of his life. On the first day of school, he got lost twice while changing classes. He was never able to figure out his locker combination and had unknowingly sat down at the "9th grade table" at lunch. By the end of the first week he had become the target of ninth graders' harassment and when his parents complained to the vice principal, Danny was called to the office by an intercom summons that was heard by his entire homeroom. He was miserable and frightened because that day he had also lost his math book with a week's assignments in it.

On the second Friday as he began to leave the building after the last bell, he was grabbed by three ninth graders who held him upside down over a toilet and threatened to "flush him down the drain." When Danny finally arrived home, he stated loudly that he was never returning to school! And who could blame him?

In the twenty years I have been in youth ministry, I have met many young people with stories similar to Danny's. When we gather Quicksilvers into our youth programs, Danny is there. We should be providing an environment that will counteract the trauma that young people experience at school. They need sanctuary. They need a place where they feel safe and welcome to interact with peers, especially older peers. They need the mentoring of a caring older teen so that bad experiences will not dominate their attitudes toward school and relationships with older peers. They need their self-esteem bolstered and they may need care-filled intervention from school administrators to help them confront bullies. They desperately need to feel safe again. Our ministry "to" youth and "for" youth must be aware of the Dannys in our midst. If we don't notice them while they are struggling with their initial attempts to adjust to new school situations, they will soon exhibit behavior that we cannot ignore.

Not all young people experience the trauma that Danny did as they move from elementary to secondary school, but the majority of Quicksilvers experience some kind of school-related stress.

## Why School Causes Stress

Our nation's schools are presently organized around developmental periods. Thus we have elementary, middle, junior high, and high schools. Fifth grade to ninth grade youngsters often spend their school day in an environment supposedly designed for their unique developmental needs, but which in reality resembles a "watered-down" version of high school.

In elementary school, young people enjoy a relative sense of security because a majority of their time is spent in self-contained, one-teacher classrooms. This security is disrupted when they move on to what are generally much larger middle or junior high schools. Almost overnight, the young people are expected to interact with not one, but often five or six different teachers. These teachers, who are primarily concerned with control, early on assign a substantial amount of academic work. A Quicksilver's day includes contact with an increased number of adults, but also with two to five times as many peers as in elementary school. As the youngest in the school, they are in an ironic situation. They may get some "TLC" from the administration for the first few days of school, but they are often the objects of derision of upper classes. They find themselves overwhelmed by an increasingly demanding academic load. They are in a frighteningly paradoxical situation. Excited to be out of elementary school, something they have looked forward to for years, they can grow to dread their daily lives at school.

Sometimes their self-esteem suffers. Whereas they may have earlier displayed great confidence in themselves, their behavior begins to exhibit the stress that permeates their lives. They may, for the first time in their lives, experience alienation, feel discounted and totally unimportant.

In the early part of this century, educators began to realize that grammar schools housing grades one through eight was not an adequate setting for dealing with puberty and the other rapidly changing developmental issues that affect the behavior, abilities, and learning styles of young adolescents.

The opening of junior high schools in their time, and now of middle schools, has been justified on grounds of the primary changes of early adolescence. The growth spurt and the onset of puberty were used as arguments for the removal of seventh and eighth graders from elementary schools. And, given that the age of pubertal onset has decreased over the past decades, the same rationale is appearing for the creation of middle schools that place sixth and sometimes fifth graders in separate buildings with seventh and eighth graders. Individual differences in the onset, duration and termination of the pubertal growth cycle often are cited as the foundation for decisions about what grade levels belong together.[7]

Unfortunately, this rationale for separation has not worked in reality. Many school districts are affected by economic and space constraints. They tend to ignore developmental issues characteristic of young adolescents when they make decisions. As a result, young adolescents attend schools that are often overcrowded, understaffed, and unequipped to handle their unique needs.

Advocacy has become a crucial service of my own ministry to Quicksilvers. I don't hesitate to call school administrators, teachers, counselors, and coaches who are usually very willing to help with young people's special needs.

Recently a junior high vice principal asked me to help him generate ideas for programs for peer counseling in his school. "I am tired of being only the disciplinarian," he said. "I want to serve these kids, not just punish them all the time. I want them to enjoy school and regard it as an important place in their lives. I want the ninth graders to regard the seventh graders as important people in this school community and not just scapegoats for their own frustrated attempts to control and overpower someone else. I would love to turn this school around so that it is not your 'typical junior high zoo,' as the teachers jokingly refer to it, but rather a place that genuinely regards kids as individuals and people of value."

We often forget that we are not only called to bring the "good news" to young people and their parents, but also to affirm the attempts of teachers and administrators to do the same. Many of the adults who staff our schools are there because they genuinely like young people, have a gift for teaching, and want to serve their community by sharing this gift. Working together with school officials, we can explore ways all of us can better address the unique needs of Quicksilvers.

**The Influence of the Media**
Recently I met with 15 high school seniors and asked them what they remembered as the greatest problem in junior-high. They unanimously agreed that "fitting in" caused them the greatest stress as young adolescents. "What do you have to do to fit in?" I asked. "You have to wear the right kind of clothes, have the right hair style, and get in with the right crowds," one young woman replied. "Who decides what kind of clothes?" I asked. The group was silent for a moment and finally one young man spoke. "I guess we are manipulated by the media to believe that certain clothes, shoes, and other products will make us more popular. And the bad thing is, it works, especially when you're in junior high," he said.

This conversation confirmed what I have long believed. The entertainment, advertising, and media industries shape our young people's attitudes about what's valuable in life, and very often these attitudes are counter-Christian.

Youth buying power represents a huge market for big business. Teenagers, in general, don't have to pay for their food and shelter, so the money they have is "throw-away" money. By some estimates they represent an annual source of approximately $13 billion in disposable income![8] Young people have become a central target of marketing research and many advertisers purposely aim their "pitch" at teenage audiences.

I asked the same group of seniors, "What do teenagers spend their money on?" Their top five answers were: 1) clothes, 2) music tapes and CDs, 3) entertainment: eating out (pizza #1), renting videos, attending films, 4) automobile expenses (gasoline, car payment, insurance), and 5) jewelry and make-up. With the exception of the automobile expenses, these choices are exactly the same for the Quicksilvers I have interviewed for this study!

Let's look closer at one of these answers: music tapes and CDs. A pattern of hero-worship is prevalent among young people in today's society. Youth under the age of 18 often idolize rock singers. It's not unusual for a teen to "adopt" a music celebrity and regard this person as a close, personal friend. Intimate knowledge is gained by reading everything available on the star's life, likes and dislikes. The young person collects tapes or CDs and countless photographs and posters and spends hours fantasizing about a relationship with the celebrity.

This typical adolescent behavior helps the young person to experience "intimacy at a distance." In other words, the young person imagines a relationship with the other without a true giving of "self," imitates the dress and habits of the admired one, and "tries on" the values espoused by the celebrity. Young people are thus investigating who they are by mirroring the characteristics they admire in their hero or heroine.

**Capitalizing on Their Admiration**
The media and advertising sectors of the business world capital-

ize on this adoration by exploiting the profitability of the celebrity and overdosing the public with products endorsed by the star. This practice heightens the interest of the young and increases the longevity of the popularity of the celebrity.

Every year the *World Almanac* surveys 5000 teenagers from all over the country who are asked to name their top ten "most admired" people in society. The top four in the results of the 1990 survey were: Paula Abdul, Mom, Michael Jordan, and Dad.

Paula Abdul presently enjoys a high degree of exposure by the media. Recently I spent an evening viewing several hours of television programs. In the time I spent in that one evening, I counted five commercials that featured Paula Abdul. Naturally her ads were all for products popular with teenagers.

This constant exposure during prime time reinforces for adolescents the idea that this heroine is someone of great importance in society. This situation can perpetuate a vicious cycle: the young's adoration is affirmed by the continual presence of the celebrity in the media, and advertisers are rewarded by an increase in the sales of their products. The higher the sales, the more the star is pursued for further media exposure. This situation continues until the star loses favor with the young, usually within five to seven years.

The ramifications of this phenomena are far-reaching. The present-day heroes of our young people are sending fictitious messages to our youth because their lives, desires, and possessions are the figments of some writer or advertising executive's imagination. As a result, our young people are enticed by the star's media exposure to become un-informed consumers. This current media trend subtly pressures the young to buy certain goods, behave certain ways, and to adopt particular images of what makes one "fit in." Young people do not generally have life experiences and a perspective that helps them recognize that they are being manipulated. And even when they recognize this manipulation, they do not generally have the ego-strength to turn their backs on it, because "it works!"

This is an area of challenge for our ministry with Quicksilvers. Many values espoused by the media are counter-Christian and tend to reinforce negative pressures on young adolescents. Yet our young people integrate these patterns of behavior, fashion styles, and music trends into their lives and make them an integral part of their sub-culture. We must honor that sub-culture's subtleties while challenging elements of it that conflict with Christian values.

The stresses and pressures faced by Quicksilvers are very real and can't be ignored as we attempt to develop ministerial goals for them. The negative impact of these stresses and pressures calls for an intentional effort on our part to counter media messages and to develop ways to help our Quicksilvers experience the "good news" of the gospels in their day-to-day lives.

## Notes

1. David Elkind, *All Grown Up and No Place to Go* (Reading, Mass.: Addison-Wesley Publishing Co., 1980), pp. 33-34.

2. Ibid., p. 36.

3. John Schwartz, "Portrait of a Generation," *Newsweek*. Special Issue: "How Kids Grow." Summer 1991, p. 6.

4. John Darcy, *Adolescents Today*, p. 181.

5. Kathleen McCoy, "Help Your Child Beat Peer Pressure," *Reader's Digest*, May 1991, pp. 67-70.

6. This case story first appeared in an article I wrote for PACE 19, entitled: "Quicksilvers: A Challenge," Spring, 1990.

7. John P. Hill, *Understanding Early Adolescence: A Framework* (Carrboro, N.C.: Center for Early Adolescence, 1980), p. 32.

8. Butch Ekstrom, "Youth Culture and Teen Spirituality, Signs of the Times," *Occasional Papers in Youth Ministry* (Naugatuck, Conn.: Center for Youth Ministry Development, 1985), p. 30.

Chapter 4

## What Critical Issues Do Quicksilvers Face?

# Self-Esteem, Substance Abuse, Sexuality, Suicide

This chapter will look at critical issues that our young adolescents encounter as they negotiate through their quicksilver years. Many of the problems they face today are problems that people 25 years ago faced in their late teens or college years.

> There's much more stress on young people than there used to be. It's a tragedy. Never before have we had a better understanding of child development or as many resources available and yet we see more troubled youth with more severe problems than ever before.[1]

Adults who work with adolescents often look at self-esteem as the most noticeable indicator of how well youth are coping with their stresses and pressures. The better adolescents feel about themselves, experts say, the less likely they are to engage in compensating behaviors that are negative and sometimes dangerous.
 In *You & Your Adolescent,* Laurence Steinberg and Ann Levine

discuss five strategies parents can use to help their teenagers build a positive self-image.[2] I offer them as valid suggestions for people in ministry who are working to raise the self-esteem of young people.

**1. Praise effort and achievement.** All people need encouragement and positive attention. Adolescents generally possess fragile egos and are emotionally vulnerable. As a result they have a genuine need for praise. I often use phrases like "Excellent job!" "Good man!" "Good woman!" when complimenting young people. It is a delight to hear those same young people compliment each other by parroting my phrases!

**2. Encourage interests and activities adolescents can master.** Quicksilvers are beginning to investigate the things that make them feel good about themselves. Each of them has some area in which he or she can excel.

**3. Give them real responsibilities.** Young people love to be needed. They have many competencies that we need to risk honoring. When they take part in projects that are other-centered, they enjoy a great sense of accomplishment and that builds their feelings of self-worth.

**4. Encourage independent thinking.** We show respect for people when we ask: "What do you think?" Quicksilvers are generally unsure of themselves and we do them a great service when we invite them to share their ideas and express their opinions. Never settle for an "I don't know." Restate the question or problem if necessary, but encourage the young person to express an opinion.

**5. Support their friendships.** We value ourselves when we discover that others value us too. Our friendships are a sign that we are approved and belong. For Quicksilvers, this is the grounding for their self-esteem.

## A Story about Angelita, age 14

Angelita is a young woman of 14 who joined our youth group this past year. She is the oldest in a four-child family and even at her vulnerable age she seems sure of herself and full of self-confidence. Her father works as a foreman in a factory and farms a small acreage. Her mother cleans houses to supplement their income and despite some economic struggles the family is strong. Angelita once told me, "Our family really cares about each other. Every night we talk about how our days went. Everyone has a turn, even my four-year-old brother. One night my dad was upset because of a possible lay-off at work. We discussed how we could all pitch in and work together to make the best of it. He didn't get laid off, but we now have enough in savings to last us quite awhile if he ever does."

Angelita's family has taken control of their lives. By some standards her family is considered poor, but their evident support and care for each other seems to help them to work as a team to face the problems that could affect all of them. They take pride in each other, and their accomplishments are celebrated by the whole family. As a family unit, they exhibit strong self-esteem, a value that is evident in Angelita's behavior.

She came to her first youth group meeting alone and joined in the activities as if she had known the other young people for years. She volunteered to organize a gathering of several youth groups in our area and seemed eager to become more involved in our monthly activities. Within three months she was one of the more active, visible youth in the parish.

Angelita is an excellent example of a person who possesses self-esteem. She is comfortable with herself and projects pervasive feelings of self-worth. She seems to value herself as a person who counts, as a competent person who has something to offer society. She likes herself and she is pleasant to be around.

Angelita and other young people like her are not just an asset to youth ministry, they are a necessity! Their positive attitudes and abilities to remain optimistic even when life is adverse is a crucial witness to other young people who find life burdensome.

Unfortunately adolescents like Angelita are rare. Low self-esteem is characteristic of most adolescents, especially those in the quicksilver years. Changes caused by puberty can throw them into a "no-control" stage of life. Self-esteem is dependent on how much we value or devalue ourselves and having some control over our "selves" affects that valuing.

Young people with dangerously low self-esteem are uncomfortable with themselves. They experience profound feelings of worthlessness and are unsure of themselves. They feel unlovable and they distrust those who profess to like and admire them. They generally feel "bad." Young people who exhibit extremely low self-regard are at great risk for self-destructive behaviors. Hope, the one Christian element that should pervade all our lives, is often totally absent from theirs. People without hope tend to devalue life itself and they adopt harmful coping mechanisms.

This leads us to critical issues that all adolescents face but that are particularly critical issues for those with low self-esteem. These are: substance abuse, premature sexual activity, and suicide.

### Dealing with Substance Abuse

"Just Say No!" has become the catch-word of the decade. Celebrities and government officials lend their names and endorsements to programs that promise prevention for drug use among the young. Their efforts seem to be having some success with all drugs except alcohol. Many studies and government figures show that in the past 25 years there has been a steady rise in the numbers of teenagers who drink. A study made by the National Institute on Drug Abuse, completed almost ten years ago, discovered that as many as 90 percent of high school seniors used alcohol during their senior year.[3] Recent studies show that this figure has not declined; some estimate that one in four 13 year olds have tried alcohol.[4]

Adolescents themselves report that drinking is prevalent among all their age groups. "By eighth grade most of our parties had some kind of drinking," state two 15-year-old girls I interviewed for this study. "When you go to a party you can almost bet there will be beer or wine coolers. There's a lot of pressure from the other kids to drink and since it's expected and accepted that you will drink, all the kids do."

Because alcohol abuse isn't always viewed seriously, I fear that its use among adolescents is the most overlooked, ignored, and neglected problem area that affects them today. Parents are usually relieved to find out that their child is drinking rather than "doing drugs." Young people themselves see nothing wrong with alcohol consumption among their peers and in fact, they regard it as one way of expressing their emerging adulthood. Law enforcement officials often turn their backs on the drinking habits of the young, unless they're called out to a rowdy drinking party. Many adults, though fearful, expect their youngsters to consume alcohol at events like proms and graduations. Some even provide the space for the parties so they can control the drinking and driving of at least their own children. Commercials romanticize beer and wine. They have a unanimously high appeal among the adolescents I talk to, and I wonder if the industry deliberately targets that audience.

Drinking is for the most part socially acceptable and, at least in this country, the age limits for legalized consumption are considered a determinant of maturity. "Adolescents and adults use the drinking age as the single most important hallmark of having achieved adult status."[5]

Unfortunately most young people regard drinking as a rite of passage, and for many of them it has become a pathway to destruction. A noticeable growing trend among medical facilities around this country is their addition of treatment programs for substance abuse. Many of these programs now specialize in adolescent patients. My own community of 50,000 people has two hospitals that include an adolescent unit in their treatment programs.

Quicksilvers, whose bodies are still growing, are at great risk of chemical addiction to alcohol. Their personal fables (discussed in the previous chapter) can lead them to ignore messages about the harmful effects of alcohol on their bodies and the dangers of addiction.

In my 20 years of working with adolescents, I have encountered many troubled youth, the majority of whom have problems related to alcohol abuse. I am concerned that this abuse is a pattern that is more prevalent than we'll admit, with consequences we are already observing. Quicksilvers and high school aged adolescents who have problems at home and in school, or who have premature sexual relationships, almost always have problems with alcohol. By the time young people are 16 and have access to cars, many have established drinking habits. Despite the laws of our country, liquor is available and readily obtainable by teenagers. "If we want it, we can get it," is the unanimous response when I ask young people how they get their weekend supply. This alarms me because more and more Quicksilvers are telling tales of heavy use and abuse among their peers.

**A Story about Billy, age 17**
I began drinking when I was nine. My father had me for the whole summer and I helped in the pit for his car racing crew. He would give me a beer when everyone would sit around the tracks drinking late at night. The first time I got drunk it was a game to my dad and his friends to see how many beers they could give me before I got sick. They thought it was funny. I thought I was one of the big guys. I drank every weekend that summer. By the time I started school again I would look for beer in the refrigerator and take one when my parents were out. I don't think I was addicted then but this kept up for a few years. By the time I was 13 I really had a problem. By then I was drinking every night and could get beer myself through a friend's sister. She'd buy me a case at a time. I hid it in the garage.

It's funny that I never had any school problems. I was on the student council, on the soccer team, and in the honor society. Somehow I never drank enough to get completely out of control.

I liked the taste of beer and I liked the way I felt when I "got a buzz on."

One day my mom came home early from work and caught me after I had had a couple of beers. She freaked out and called my step-dad home from work. They both sat down with me and gave me the old lecture and grounding. They never asked me where I got it, if I had any more or how long this had gone on. I think they just hoped it was a one-time deal. I was only in seventh grade so I guess they figured it couldn't be too bad at that age. I just got better at hiding my drinking and they never caught me again.

Within a couple more years it got so bad that I was taking it to school. In 9th grade, my best friend got sick of it and told me off one day. You have to understand, he's been my best friend since third grade and he is still my best friend. He told me if I didn't stop drinking and ruining my life, he was never going to see me again. I got p———off at him and told him to get out of my life. We didn't talk for two weeks, but I couldn't stand it any more. One night I went over to his house real late and we talked for hours. The next night he went to an AA meeting with me.

I've been sober for two years now. It's been the hardest thing I have ever had to do. I still go to parties and I can't say if I'll never drink again. I just take one day at a time.

What I really appreciate are the times I can be with other kids where there isn't any booze. Youth group has been important for me. At least I can see kids having a good time without drinking. The only weekend I was sober in eighth grade was on the church ski trip. I didn't want my youth minister to find out and have to send me home. I really liked her and I was afraid she would hate me. I almost went nuts, but I purposely skied hard all day so that I would just fall into bed at night. I didn't drink and I found out I could be sober. That helped me when I finally went to AA.

My advice to adults who are worried about kids and alcohol is to talk to them about it and have kids like me talk to them, especially junior high kids. No one ever told me what could happen and no one ever told me I had a problem until my friend confronted me. I wish I had heard about how bad it could be when I was in junior high. All I ever heard was what was good about it.

If it wasn't for my best friend, I'd probably be a drunken bum by now. The things that help me the most now are him and his encouragement, my AA group, and God. I pray a lot because I know I can't do this alone. It's scary to think I have a lot of life left and I already have a big problem. I am an alcoholic and I am not even out of high school yet!"

**Talk about Drinking**
We who are involved with young people should talk to them about drinking, and we should provide an environment that is alcohol free. Youth groups should never meet in places where drinking is permitted, even among the sponsors. Adults who sponsor youth events should remember that they are there for young people, not to entertain themselves. "To be one of the big guys," as Billy said, is one of the motivators for young people to start drinking. As adults we have an awesome responsibility. Young people learn by imitating us. We are the mirrors for their behavior and it is important for them to experience fun-filled times with us, times when there is no drinking.

Young people need to know that we care about them and their welfare, and that we want what's best for them. When we make rules for our youth events regarding alcohol or drug use, we must set realistic consequences and follow through on them. Youth need and want our guidance, and it may be our rules that give them the strength to "just say no!"

Prevention programs in high school come too late. Still anxious and willing to discuss their life issues with adults, Quicksilvers are at a stage of development where they need and desire adult approval. Older teens who have dealt with the issues of parties, drinking, and peer pressure should be invited to talk to the younger ones about their experiences. No thanks to the adults in his life during his quicksilver years, Billy is a success story. It was a peer who confronted him. It is often peers who know the extent of the drinking, and it is often peers who can help the most. Peer ministry is an important component to any effective youth ministry program. Older youth are usually very willing to talk to and partner off with younger ones to discuss the "good and bad" times of growing up. Many parishes and Catholic schools use this kind of programming very effectively to orient young adolescents to youth group or high school experiences.

**Premature Sexual Activity**
One of the greatest changes in puberty is heightened sexual awareness. The bodies of Quicksilvers are in constant physical turmoil as hormonal surges join with rapid growth to produce a restlessness that is evident in their constant-motion behavior. Combine these new erotic urges with media titillation and alcohol use and we have youth-at-risk for premature sexual activity. Statistics indicate that sexual activity among adolescents now involves younger and younger teens. The numbers are unbelievably alarming!

"One in five youngsters under 15 say they have had sexual intercourse," reports a survey of 8000 young adolescents done by the Search Institute.[6] Dating habits of early adolescents emulate those of older teens a decade ago. The pregnancy rate for unmarried teenagers has not declined but increased in the past five years. Premature sexual activity has steadily moved to a younger age, and those under the age of 16 are at the greatest risk for sexually transmitted diseases and pregnancy because they do not have the maturity to practice "safe sex."

Why is this happening and what can we do to meet the challenge? Let me suggest two larger factors currently operating in young people's lives that make meeting this challenge so intimidating.

First, young people are gaining many of their moral values regarding sexuality in overt messages from the media. These blatantly imply that sexual intercourse is the usual way to express intimacy in a relationship.

Reflect with me a moment on the last film you saw. What was the sexual relationship of the main characters? Were they married? To each other? When was the last time you saw a film where unmarried couples did not have intimate sexual activity as part of their relationship?

Listen to the words of the latest top ten songs. (It doesn't matter if it's hard rock, rap, or country.) Do any of the lyrics equate committed relationship with physical expressions of intimacy? How many of the songs hint at exploitation of another for one's own pleasure?

Sit and watch television for two hours, especially prime time or afternoon soap operas. "Who is sleeping with whom?" is a common conversation topic of young teens. Young people are getting a continuous subliminal message from the media that sexual intimacy is the common way to relate in dating.

Even commercials use erotic images and sexual innuendoes to sell products. They are not just selling perfume or cologne or automobiles or designer jeans, they are also selling sex! And our young people are buying it. They are not aware that they are being enticed into activities for which they are not physically or emotionally prepared.

We need to challenge this media message and one way is to discuss with young people the ramifications of the subliminal effect the media's message has on their sexual practices. We can offer honest assessments of the negative aspects of premature sex. We can stress the positive aspects of relating to others in non-physical ways for more healthy dating practices. We can compare the message of the media with the message of the gospel in carefully planned discussions to help young people see that the media message endorses a morality that is not acceptable to young Christians. We have a responsibility as Christian ministers to help our young discover that sexuality is best and most completely experienced when it is understood as a sacred and precious gift from God.

Second, we are not, today, saying to young people what was

said to us when we were young: that virginity and abstinence are viable options for sexual relationships.

That wise message is still a good one. Our sexuality is a gift from our creator. It may be the most important gift of "self" that we have to share with another. Intimacy demands maturity and commitment. We need to tell our young people that having sex with someone is giving the most special gift we have. Once given, it can never be taken back. Delaying sex is a true sign that we love someone and are not using them for our own pleasure or allowing them to use us.

Young people in a ministry program, whether it be education, social, or spiritual, have a right to hear a positive message about sexuality within the context of Christian morality. Young people need our input and wisdom so they can recognize the materialistic reasons behind the media's emphasis on sex as a way to sell their products.

**Techniques That Help**
In the eighth- and ninth-grade human sexuality units of my parish religion classes, we practice several techniques to combat media influences. At the end of each class in a three week unit on human sexuality, we incorporate time for the participants to jot down any questions they have about sex. The questions are collected and reviewed by the teaching team who prepare answers before the next meeting. Almost without exception during the past six years, several young people have asked, "When is it okay to have sex?"

Our teaching team reinforces a commitment to the grounding principle that premature sex is not healthy for young people either physically or emotionally. Our presumption is that the consequences of premature sex are never positive for them, and we try to lead participants into an understanding of this important concept.

Positive decision making is a necessary skill in dealing with this issue. The following guidelines, designed by Bob McCarty of the Archdiocese of Baltimore's Office of Youth Ministry, provide an excellent discussion tool for conversations with Quicksilvers on sexual behavior. These guidelines were actually drawn up with assistance from a group of high school students.

**1. Know the facts.** Do not ignore or minimize risks involved. Famous lines like "It can't happen to me..." or "You can't get pregnant the first time..." are just that, lines. Pregnancy, AIDS, and venereal diseases are real.

**2. Maintain perspective.** Remember everyone, at whatever age, thinks they are "mature enough." Having sex is no indication of maturity. Maturity is reflected in good decision making.

**3. Ask yourself:** "If I do whatever it is I am considering, will I have any regret later if we stop going together?" (The odds are that this will happen sooner or later.) Intercourse is an irreversible communication. What kind of memories will you have of this sexual encounter? Do you see yourself with this person next month? Next year? In five years?

**4. Ask yourself:** "Am I using someone? Am I being used? Am I doing what I think is expected of me?" Even though you might think "Everyone does it," ask yourself, "Who is everyone?" and "Does that make it right for me?"

**5. Learn how to relax** and enjoy your sexual feelings. Know your sexual limits and communicate them clearly. Don't expect your date to have E.S.P.

**6. Be honest**—with yourself and with your friend—every step of the way. What does your relationship mean now, and what do you want it to mean? What are you communicating nonverbally? If you can't talk about it, don't do it. If you can't ask questions, perhaps it's because you are afraid of the answers.

**7. Consider what others have to say.** Learn from the experiences of others. Talk to your parents, teachers, and other trusted adults and don't let anyone pressure you or make up your mind. Decide in favor of giving sex the most meaning possible for yourself, regardless of what others say or do.

**8. Sex is not a strong enough bond** to permanently hold a relationship together, so don't count on it. Never use sex to cement a relationship. The famous line is "If you loved me, you would...." A good response is "If you loved me, you wouldn't pressure me to do something I'm not ready for." Never use sex to prove love, and never use sex to get love.

9. **If you find yourself wondering, "Is it okay for me?"** it is not okay. The fact that you asked yourself the question means that it's not okay. When sex is right for you, you will have no serious doubts.

10. **Waiting is the Christian option.** It is always safe to wait. As teenagers we are emotionally vulnerable and often confused about relationships and sexuality. The church teaches in favor of waiting for the permanent commitment of marriage. And remember, it is always possible to re-evaluate and change the pattern of our behavior or relationships, especially if we think we have jumped into too much, too soon.[7]

The issue of premature sex among teenagers is one of the most crucial areas of morality that faces the church. Our dealings with Quicksilvers on this issue need to be tempered by a conscious effort to assure them that we offer love and concern, not judgment.

### Suicide and Teenagers

The suicide rate for teenagers has tripled over the last 25 years, and the rate for 10-14 year olds has increased 166 percent. Each year, approximately 5000 teenagers kill themselves. Suicide is the second leading cause of death among young people under the age of 20, second only to automobile accidents.[8] Many law enforcement officials feel that some road accidents may also be disguised suicides.

Nothing is more devastating to those left behind than the suicide of an adolescent. Any death of a young person seems unnatural, but a suicide always makes survivors feel they have failed. Parents, the young person's friends, others in the community wonder if they bear part of the blame. This is the ultimate "no win" situation. Guilt is inexplicably interwoven with grief. "Why" is the constant question posed, and there is no acceptable answer. This death should not have been.

Grief ministry is crucial for all those involved. The parents need someone to sit with them while they cry, articulate their guilt, and express their frustrations over the senselessness of their child's death. The young friends desperately need a process for discussing their confusion and anger so that they do not turn it inward on themselves. The community needs to publicly express its sadness and disappointment that the young suicide victim saw no other way out when there may have been many possible solutions. And counselors, teachers, and ministers should come forward to help other youth who might be considering the same action.

Young people who take their own lives rarely do so without first sending warning signals. The typical suicide victim is lonely, severely depressed, has extremely low self-esteem, and often has some drug or alcohol involvement. Many lack opportunities to express their unhappiness and are frustrated by feelings of failure and hopelessness. Usually they don't want to die, they just want to change their lives. A successful juvenile suicide is a cry for help that has backfired!

Identification of these troubled youth and taking immediate preventive measures may be the only way we can circumvent such tragedies. A survey on teenage suicide conducted by the Gallup International Institute (in the winter of 1991) revealed that of the 1152 teenagers interviewed, 47 percent felt that if a friend was considering suicide, he or she could get help, and a member of the clergy would be someone from whom they would seek help; 89 percent felt churches should offer counseling to prevent teenagers from committing suicide. Only 28 percent of those surveyed felt that their churches were presently doing anything to prevent teenage suicides.[9]

I have found a quiet reluctance on the part of adolescents to discuss this issue openly with their peers. They are frightened and they feel inadequate to the task of counseling a friend whom they suspect might be considering suicide. One technique I find helpful is to discuss with them the early warning signs, things to do and things not to do when they suspect the danger of suicide. This information gives them some sense of direction and control.

The following lists are provided by the Center for Early Adolescence, and were originally designed for adults, parents, and teachers. I have adapted them for use with young adolescents.

**Early Warning Signs**
1. The person says things like: "I wish I were dead." "Everybody would be better off without me." "There is nothing to live for."
2. If you know your friend has tried to commit suicide before, you know they are at risk.
3. Your friend is preoccupied with death in music, art, and personal writing.
4. Your friend has lost a family member, pet, or boy or girl friend through death, abandonment, or break-up.
5. Your friend's family has been disrupted by unemployment, serious illness, or divorce.
6. Your friend reports disturbances in sleeping and eating habits.
7. Your friend starts giving away his or her prized possessions.
8. Your friend has no regard for his or her personal safety.

**What to Do**
1. Ask a straightforward question like "Are you thinking about hurting yourself?" Ask in a calm manner.
2. Listen and be supportive.
3. As soon as you can, tell someone else. Encourage your friend to talk to an adult who can help.
4. Try to determine how serious your friend is. Ask questions about feelings, personal relationships, who else the person has

talked to and the amount of thought he or she has given to the means to be employed. If a gun, pills, rope or other means are available, the situation is very dangerous. Inform some adult immediately! If possible, stay with your friend or keep your friend on the phone until you can get an adult's help.

**What Not to Do**
1. Do not ignore warning signals.
    2. Do not react with horror, disapproval, or repulsion.
    3. Do not make false promises like "Everything will be all right."
    4. Do not give simple answers or criticisms like "You should be thankful for...." "Don't be a jerk, you won't kill yourself."

Conversations and discussions on this topic empower the majority of teens to feel more comfortable with their role in prevention, but they also provide an opportunity to get help for those who may be contemplating suicide themselves.

**A Story about Carla, age 14**
Our junior high youth had just seen and discussed the film *Inside, I Ache*[10] when one of the adult leaders approached me about Carla. "Carla came up to me with tears in her eyes and said she needed to talk to someone about a 'friend' who was thinking of suicide," reported the adult. "She is waiting outside your office now to talk to you."

Carla was very eager to tell me that her "friend" was feeling pretty rotten about herself. She had just been dumped by her boyfriend; her grades had all dropped during the last month; she had not made the basketball team and the night before she had been caught by her parents sneaking into the house after a drinking party. Her parents were furious with her and she was sure they would come "totally unglued" when they got her report card. Carla's conversational style as she narrated these events soon switched into the first person. I did not stop her and soon she gave me an opening when she said, "I just don't feel like living any more." When I gently asked her if she was the one thinking about suicide, she admitted with relief that she was.

Carla wanted to talk. She was depressed and scared, but she was not in despair. She wanted to regain the trust and approval of her parents and she wanted to do better in school. Would she have attempted suicide? Since it's impossible to say, we who counsel youth must provide opportunities for them to discuss that most terrible of possibilities. If we can find ways to open the dialogue about suicide between peers, we at least help to remove the cloak of secrecy that inhibits healthy, probing, provocative and, we hope, healing talk.

Through four months of counseling Carla rallied emotionally and began to improve in all areas of her life. She did not have an addiction problem, and she had parents willing to go into counseling, two great benefits many Quicksilvers don't have in similar crisis situations.

Young people like Carla can easily slip into despair when they feel hopeless and helpless. As church ministers we have a responsibility to listen attentively for their cries for help. If they consider suicide an option to avoid the pain in their lives, we must must offer alternative ways to deal with that pain and to offer them hope and support.

The critical issues I have addressed in this chapter are all issues in my own ministerial efforts with adolescents. They are frightening, but they won't go away overnight. We must face them and deal with them. They will continue to be a part of our challenge to effectively share the "good news" of Jesus with today's young.

## Notes

1. Dr. John Stephenson, pediatrician and medical director of the University of Wisconsin, Madison Teen Clinic. Quoted in *The Capitol Times*, "The Disappearance of Childhood" by Jacob Stockinger, staff writer.

2. Laurence Steinberg and Ann Levine, *You & Your Adolescent* (New York: Harper & Row, 1990), pp. 146-147.

3. Barbara Schneider Fuhrmann, *Adolescence, Adolescents* (Boston: Little, Brown & Company, 1986), p. 472.

4. Laurence Steinberg and Ann Levine, ibid., p. 119.

5. Fuhrmann, ibid., p. 477.

6. Peter L. Benson, et al., *The Quicksilver Years: The Hopes and Fears of the Early Adolescent* (San Francisco: Harper & Row, 1986), p. 58.

7. Bob McCarty.

8. David Elkind, *All Grown Up and No Place to Go* (Reading, Mass.: Addison-Wesley Publishing Co., 1984), p. 188, and Laurence Steinberg and Ann Levine, ibid., p. 414.

9. *Emerging Trends*, "The Role of the Churches in Teen Suicide," May 1991. Published by Princeton Religion Research Center.

10. *Inside, I Ache* is an excellent film to use with young adolescents and their parents. It is distributed by Mass Media Ministries, Baltimore, Maryland.

Chapter 5

*How Do Quicksilvers Grow in Faith?*

# Evangelization: Invitation, Catechesis, Conversion

The call came late one afternoon as I prepared to leave the parish for the day. It was the chaplain at one of the adolescent treatment centers calling to ask if I could visit a young person in the hospital who wanted to talk to a Catholic. I met Randy in the hospital cafeteria and we began our first of many visits. "This is my third time in treatment," he said, "and I want to do it right this time because I think God has some plan for me." "Oh, why do you think that?" I asked. He began a story that astounded me in terms of the amount of trauma he had endured in a brief 15 years of life. Here is his story.

I have been in foster care since I was 18 months old. Every time I thought I had found a family I could call my own, my real parents would reappear and I would go back to live with them for awhile. The best time of all those years was when I was nine. I stayed with my grandparents for almost a year. My grandfather was Catholic and sometimes he would take me to church with him.

I remember the first time very well. My grandfather came to me on Saturday and told me he had something special planned. He told me he would be honored if I would go to church with him. His church was having a special children's program and he wanted to take me to it. I think it was some kind of a Halloween celebration. All the kids were dressed up in costumes and we sat on the floor around the priest and he told us stories about Jesus. It was lots of fun and I felt like the priest was telling the stories just to me.

On the way home my grandfather rephrased what the priest had said: "Jesus can see through your masks and loves you no matter what you look like underneath them. No matter what you look like or where you live or who you are, Jesus loves you." I don't know why I always remember my grandfather telling me that, but I do!

At the end of that year something terrible happened. My dad shot and killed my mother and my grandparents, and I went back into a foster home. I was really messed up after that. I started drinking when I was ten and doing drugs when I was 12. I ended up being moved from one foster home to another. No one could control me and I stopped counting how many homes I'd been in after about eleven. My social worker tried to put me in a group home last year and when they were moving me from the hospital to the home, I jumped out of a three story window.

I wasn't really trying to kill myself; I thought there was a fire escape out there. Anyway I fell onto concrete steps, crushed both of my ankles and broke my back in two places. At first they didn't think I would live and then they didn't think I would walk again. But here I am, bent up like an old man, but alive, and I can walk. I really think God has plans for me, or else I would have died. I want to know more about God and the Catholic church. I'd kinda like to be a part of a church that teaches about love because I need that.

Randy is one of society's throwaway children. In many ways he is considered by others to be insignificant and unimportant.

God cares about Randy but Randy only has an inkling of that reality. He needs evangelization. His grandfather began the initial movements of evangelization by inviting Randy to investigate the Catholic community of faith. Randy now desperately needs to continue his healing process. His grandfather's invitation to "come and see" laid the groundwork for Randy's request for conversation with someone from the church.

**Bringing Them to God**
Evangelization has had "bad press" among Catholics. We have defined it only as "going door-to-door trying to convince people to join our church." But this image does not at all portray the essence of evangelization, which literally means to preach the gospel. The story about Randy and his grandfather illustrates much more closely what evangelization is and should be.

The best evangelization begins with a one-on-one relationship. To initiate these relationships, we must sometimes go where our young people are. Where are they in today's society? How can we, possibly significant adults in their lives, find them to begin the process of sharing the good news of the gospel with them?

They are in the middle schools and junior highs in our communities. On weekends they are in the malls. On summer evenings they are at the local playgrounds and parks, and on weekday afternoons, mostly unsupervised, they are hanging around the house waiting for their working parents to come home. Usually this age group is eager for something to do. Opening our churches, youth rooms, gymnasiums, and recreation areas after school is one way to attract them to "come and see."

Of course, it is easy to begin relationships with the ones who do come to us, to the church or youth ministry programs, but what should we be doing about the ones who don't show up? The Randys in our lives are rare. He took the initiative. We must reach out to others like him: the young people who are at risk, unchurched, and marginalized. They are "out there" and we must look for them. They are the true targets of the gospel mandate from Matthew 28:19: "Go, therefore, make disciples of all nations; baptize them in the name of the Father, and of the Son, and of the Holy Spirit, and teach them to observe all the commands I gave you." They are the most needy and neglected of our young, and they hunger for the power of the gospel message that says they are significant and important.

**We Must Invite Them**
Invitation is our first action in the evangelization process. To be successful, we must sometimes leave our comfortable environments and approach the turf that is familiar and comfortable to young people. Jeff Johnson, one of the pioneers of modern Youth Ministry, calls this kind of activity "movement from neutral turf to holy ground." He says, "When we are on neutral turf, relationships can happen more easily, without roles, especially authority roles. Young people are attracted to real human beings, not adults playing roles."[1] This is where true evangelization happens. In a sense, then, our challenge is to go "door-to-door." But our movement to neutral turf is not for the purpose of coercion. It is motivated by the desire to share the good news, simply to offer friendship. We should be about sharing the incredible reality of the God who loves us! When we gather in friendship on neutral turf, with hope grounded in the gospel, we experience God's very transformation of neutral turf into holy ground.

We adventurers must also remember that acceptance is only the first step. Many of the youth who come to our programs are in need of continual evangelization; they have responded to our invitation to come but have not yet heard the good news. Randy's grandfather completed the first action in evangelization and attempted to move on. He explained the gospel message to his grandson in a way that made sense to Randy. In fact his sharing of the message of Jesus' unconditional love was a message that Randy carried with him through the most traumatic six years of his life.

The second action in evangelization is to present the gospel to the young people in our lives, to the *unchurched* as well as the *churched*.

When we refer to the "unchurched," we are identifying two important characteristics of many young people. The first characteristic is that many youth are "outside the faith community," perhaps due to family situation, lack of parental involvement or negative prior contact with the church.

A second characteristic of the "unchurched" is that many are within the faith community, but outside the experience of the gospel. Though they may be members of our youth programs, religious education classes, or Catholic schools, many young people have not experienced the message of Jesus in the gospel. Outreach includes the element of proclaiming the good news to those who have not experienced it.[2]

It is through continued encounters with the gospel that people begin to develop a sense of what gives life meaning and begin to experience conversion to a way of living that fosters the reign of God. Young adolescents are at a crossroads. They are eager to learn more about God, and they are ready developmentally to begin internalizing some of the faith values that have been presented to them ever since they began coming to the church and our programs.

As I said earlier, the primary psychosocial urge of Quicksilvers is to identify a group with whom to belong. Once that task is completed the young person is ready (psychologically) to investigate the values espoused by that group. It is an important challenge for us who minister to this age group to intentionally, personally, and continually invite Quicksilvers to join "our group." Only then can the church become an agent for conversion in their lives.

### A Story about Josie, age 13

Josie entered seventh grade with great excitement. She was nervous about school, but was looking forward to it, too. She was also anxious to join the parish youth group. Her older sister was an active member, and her parents had helped sponsor some previous youth events.

At Josie's first few youth meetings, everything seemed to be fine. When she refused to go to the next two events, her parents began to worry. And when she seemed hesitant about going to religion class and church, they knew something was wrong. They sat down with Josie and through conversation discovered that she felt ignored by the adults at youth group and disregarded by the other youth. She had tried to join a game at the last youth meeting, and had been blatantly excluded by some kids who told her, "Go find your own group." Josie was devastated and no longer felt welcomed at church events.

Josie's parents called the parish youth minister who realized that careful re-invitation and experiences of welcome and trust would be necessary for Josie to feel like she belonged to this group. For Josie an important element of evangelization was missing. She was invited to "come and see" and she responded eagerly. But when she arrived, she had no experience of inclusion or connectedness.

### Connections Are Important

A typical Quicksilver like Josie displays a large degree of insecurity and needs to be noticed and to feel included at every meeting. Adults must be attuned to this need and go from there.

> Connections on a personal level are vital if our young people are to genuinely feel welcomed by the church. These relationships, based on mutual trust and respect, are very important in combating the alienation that many youth feel in the church. Personal connections lead to community. Community can be described as a network of connections

in which youth have the opportunity to grow, share and celebrate together. It is within this kind of community that the gospel message is best understood.[3]

Henri Nouwen in *Reaching Out* reflects that the greatest challenge to those of us responsible for enhancing the spiritual lives of others is to practice the hospitality of Jesus who responded to others and to their most basic personal needs within a framework of friendship. We must "offer our students the place (space) where they can reveal their greatest potential to love, to give and to create, and where they can find the affirmation that gives them the courage to continue their search."[4]

Hospitality, when used effectively with Quicksilvers, should be duplicative; that is, the youth who have been the recipients of our intentional efforts at hospitality become, in turn, hospitable towards new youth who come to our programs. This posture of hospitality does not come naturally to the youth in our programs. We must sponsor their efforts to welcome each other. Their own needs for belonging can interfere with their abilities to automatically welcome others. This element of invitation is the connector that gives young people a bonding with the Christian community and an eagerness to hear the gospel. When they learn to reach out and be hospitable towards other youth, they are ready for experiences of outreach that go beyond the perimeters of the church.

## How We Share Good News

How is the evangelization process carried out and how is the good news shared? Given the particular needs of Quicksilvers, this is a vitally important question. Often the way the good news is presented to them is unexciting, lacks the ability to sustain their interest, and fails to give them the grounding they need to establish life-long growth in faith.

"The fundamental process of adolescent catechesis involves discovering the relationships among the Catholic Christian tradition; God's present activity in the life of the adolescent's family, community and world; and the contemporary life experience of the adolescent."⁵

Effective youth ministers for Quicksilvers must read the signs of the times in society as reflected in music, media, and lifestyles, and they should challenge young people to consider the often negative influence of these signs in shaping their values.

> Effective catechesis is in tune with the life situations of youth—their language, lifestyles, family realities, culture and global realities. It identifies the core meaning of the signs, symbols and the images of youth today; explores how these surface in youth's lives and relates them to the signs, symbols and images of the Catholic Christian tradition.⁶

While interviewing young people for this book, I wondered if these important principles of adolescent catechesis were being addressed around the country. The Quicksilvers I interviewed were candid about how effective they felt their catechetical programs were. I asked the following of all the young people I interviewed:

Tell me about your religion class. What do you study? What do you like or dislike about it? Why do you think it's important for the church to offer religion classes? What kinds of activities does your parish have for people your age? In what ways do you think the church cares about you? The following are two sample answers.

Our classes are held on Tuesday afternoons and we don't like that at all! The most popular club at school is held on Tuesdays after school so we are not allowed to join it this year. Mom promised that next year if the club meets on the same day as religion, we could skip religion classes for a year.

We are studying about the church and we hate to say this, but it is pretty boring. Our teachers are very strict and we have homework and tests. All we do is read from the books, do worksheets, and memorize stuff for tests. We never seem to talk about things that are interesting to us. The best thing is that there are no classes after confirmation and that's just in two more years.

It's important for the church to have religion classes because we need to know more about God and what the church teaches. We wish we could ask questions about the things we don't understand. Melissa got into a lot of trouble when she said she doesn't think the church teaches the right thing about some stuff. She just wasn't sure she understood why the church taught the way it did. We would really like to have more discussions. The classes are too much like school and they are not fun at all.

There's nothing else at our parish for kids our age. We love to have parties and dances. It seems that the only thing our church cares about is if we attend religion classes. They call our mother when we're absent. She said it's because classes are so important. We just wish they were more interesting.

—Melissa and Elena, sisters, ages 13 and 14

I take religion from my grandfather. I go to school out of town and I can't get back into town in time for the regular classes. I like what we are studying. It's all about the church and what we believe. My grandfather and I get into interesting discussions about what the church was like when he was little and what it is like now. I think it's neat that they used to speak a different language in church back then.

I like our parish; it's special. My family has gone to it all the way back to my great-great-grandparents. I was picked to be one of the special altar boys. My grandfather said it was a great honor because there are only five boys in the whole parish who are picked to do this. We serve all the special times and at the biggest Mass on Sunday mornings. The priest asked me himself if I would be one of those special servers! I like church and I like going to Mass every week. My grandfather sits in the front of the church every time I serve. I can't wait for Christmas. It will be my first Midnight Mass. I feel pretty involved at church and I can't think of anything else the church could do for kids my age.

It's important for the church to have classes because it helps the people involved in it to realize how special God is in their lives. I like learning about Jesus and talking to my grandfather about the church. I think the church cares about kids because they have special things for kids to do like serving.

—Jon, age 12, same texts, same parish

Reflect a minute on the descriptions given by these three youth and the differences in their experiences and perceptions of the church and its importance to their lives. They all come from the same economic and ethnic group. Their parents' values are basically the same, and they enjoy the stability of two-parent homes and close extended families. The extremes of their reactions are representative of the attitudes of other Quicksilvers I interviewed; they show where and how we are succeeding or not in connecting to the young adolescents in our church family.

The most apparent differences in their attitude towards their religious education is that Jon is involved in a special one-on-one relationship in both his class situation and his involvement at Mass. He has been "invited" to join a special group that gives him a significant sense of importance.

Melissa and Elena, on the other hand, feel no sense of connection to their religious education. They are neither challenged nor involved in their own learning and they are being asked to "give back" information that is "fed to them" in an unexciting and uninteresting way. They perceive their religion classes as competing with activities they value, and given the chance to choose between the two, they would choose the school club.

What an important challenge for our future ministry with Quicksilvers! Both stories illustrate the necessity to design catechetical materials that address the unique developmental needs and characteristics of young adolescents and that appreciate their growing abilities to accept Jesus' message and the traditions that Catholic Christians hold dear.

The National Federation for Catholic Youth Ministry suggests the best catechetical material for Quicksilvers focuses on particular faith themes. They list themes that address specific issues within six integral dimensions of faith: Jesus, scripture, church, prayer, action/lifestyles, and critical reflection. The themes are organized around a focus and a suggested content. For example, on the theme of "Personal Growth," they suggest the following focus and content.

**Focus:** This faith theme helps younger adolescents develop a stronger and more realistic concept of self by exploring who they are and who they can become.

**Suggested Content:** the building of a strong and realistic concept of self with an emphasis on self-concept, growing autonomy, and self-determination; Jesus' vision of being fully human and its impact on the younger adolescent's growing identity as a Christian; the response of the good news and tradition to adolescent struggles (isolation, loneliness, frustration, anger) and problems (suicide, substance abuse); the development of skills for handling peer pressure and values, and adolescent problems.[7]

Our catechetical work with Quicksilvers is critical for the future of our church. They deserve our best efforts and our finest resources. They deserve programs that acknowledge their needs on the journey towards mature faith and commitment.

### Commitment Comes Later

At a crucial moment in the evangelization process, a person makes a commitment, a conscious decision about the importance of faith and how to live out this faith in society. This commitment is usually referred to as the conversion point of the faith journey. In my opinion, it would be unusual for a Quicksilver to reach this level of faith maturity. Given the developmental characteristics of this age group, the commitment process usually comes later, but it should be our goal, the vision that guides all our ministerial efforts. We should therefore focus our energies on the initial actions of evangelization which are invitation, welcome, and an intentional sharing of our faith stories. Conversion entails transformation and a willingness to take on the responsibility of sharing the gospel with others. We share the good news because it is contagious! God loves us! We must respond!

"Religious conversion is ultimately the act of falling in love with God."[8] Love qualifies a relationship. Saint Paul, in 1 Corinthians 13, tells us that love has these characteristics: It is patient, kind, not jealous, never rude, boastful, or self-seeking; it is not snobbish, not prone to anger, not vengeful; it is filled with forbearance, trust, hope, and the power to endure. This kind of love demands a response, and it demands maturity. This kind of love must be learned and practiced. This is the grounding for the way Jesus related and taught others about God. It should be our grounding as we lead Quicksilvers toward conversion.

In the process of falling in love with God, young people need time to look for answers to their questions about life; they need to be able to express their doubts, and they need to have the freedom to search out reasons for their disbelief. They need to learn what it means to love others as themselves, and they need to practice loving in God's way. We show others that we love God by loving them as God would. This action means that we not only know how God loves, but we come to live our lives based on profound trust in God's will. This combination of knowing and trusting leads us to respond to God's love by offering service to others. This is the kind of "falling in love" that we invite Quicksilvers to when we begin the process of evangelization with them.

In her pertinent study of early adolescents, Anita M. Farel helps us make a profound connection. "Current research about early adolescence suggests that there is an important relationship between religion and adolescent development."[9] Farel's findings suggest a further connection: the beginnings of an internalization of moral standards and a coherent philosophy of life. Young adolescents continually raise questions about religious faith. They search for answers that help them make connections between their religious beliefs and their daily lives. They will readily turn to youth ministers for help in decision making and coping with problems.

This is good news for those of us who work in ministry with this age group. We are not only important for their faith development, but we are also a key factor in their journey toward mature adulthood.

**Jesus Our Model**
Through evangelization we invite the young to join our family of faith. They come and find affirmation when they experience our hospitality and welcome. They begin to trust us enough to question us about our faith, and we catechize them with stories that sustain our beliefs. These stories tell of the great love God has for us and of our greatest gift from God, Jesus, the Christ. The grounding for our faith and the model for our lifestyles is found in the story of Jesus whose life was one of total service to those he loved. We, in turn, commit our lives to others as we respond to the example of Jesus.

We invite Quicksilvers to "come and see" and we join them in encountering more deeply the object of our love who is God. This is what happened with Randy.

His grandfather began the initial steps in the evangelization process, but life circumstances placed Randy's conversion on hold. Randy had many questions about God, how God operated in his life and how he could learn more about God and Jesus. Randy had a need to be informed. We had long conversations that were on-going question and answer sessions. Randy's eagerness for knowledge was infectious. I continually read and looked for resources that might be helpful for his quest. I arrived at our sessions with arms loaded with books and tapes and articles to help facilitate our time together. He never seemed to get enough.

Randy was very interested in experiences of prayer. He genuinely wanted to communicate with God, but he wasn't sure of the ways of prayer. His approach to prayer was innocently precious. He stood before God unashamed and filled with wonder and trust. He spoke to God directly as if I weren't present. His attitude was so open and receptive that I often felt I was intruding. But he insisted I stay with him and pray with him. To this day I feel I was an invited guest at a profound moment of grace between this young man and God. It was truly an awesome experience and has remained one of the most special memories of my 20 years in youth ministry.

Randy's story continues to have a happy ending. He was placed with a nurturing, caring young couple who agreed to take over his foster care. For almost the first time in his life Randy began having experiences of affirmation. His foster parents included him in their life as active Catholic Christians. He joined a youth group and began formal religious instruction. Soon Randy requested fuller membership and was received into the church.

Randy now displays elements of readiness for commitment to the gospel. Last Christmas he led the youth group of his parish in organizing projects for the poor. He talks to younger teens about substance abuse and he is a strong advocate for needy teens. I recently overheard him explain to another youth the "whys" of his involvement in church. "God saved my life. God needs me to do these projects and God needs you too! It won't get done if we don't do it. Remember Jesus is out there with the poor. If we call ourselves followers of Jesus, then we have to help the poor even if it's not convenient because that's where we meet Jesus face-to-face!"

Randy just celebrated his sixteenth birthday. He is leaving the Quicksilver years and is ready to move smoothly through the rest of adolescence. Randy is aware that he's important to his parish, school, and community. He has been formed, informed, and is in the midst of transformation. He is a valid example of the evangelization process at its best. He has become a committed young Catholic Christian who knows he is loved and is called to go forth and love others!

### Notes

1. Jeff Johnson, "Evangelization of Youth," Occasional Paper 31 (Naugatuck, Conn.: Center for Youth Ministry Development, 1986), p. 3.

2. Robert McCarty, "Outreach: Ministry to Unchurched Youth," *Readings in Youth Ministry* (Washington, D.C.: The National Federation for Catholic Youth Ministry, 1989), p. 2.

3. Ibid., pp. 5-6.

4. Henri J.M. Nouwen, *Reaching Out* (New York: Doubleday, 1975), p. 62.

5. *The Challenge of Adolescent Catechesis* (Washington, D.C.: The National Federation for Catholic Youth Ministry, 1986), p. 9.

6. Ibid.

7. Ibid., p. 13. Other themes listed are: Church, Jesus and the Gospel Message, Morality and Moral Decision Making, Relationships, Service, and Sexuality.

8. Thomas Groome, *Sharing Faith* (New York: Harper Collins, 1991), p. 130.

9. Anita M. Farel, *Early Adolescence and Religion: A Status Study* (Carrboro, N.C.: Center for Early Adolescence, 1983), p. 17.

# Conclusion

The quicksilver years are a period of enormous change, growth, and activity. This age group needs adults who genuinely care about them and enjoy their zest for life. They need adults who also recognize the vulnerability of this time of life. With caring adults as friends and advocates, they will learn to value themselves as important members of their church and society. To the extent that we as church provide an atmosphere of acceptance and show a sincere interest in their lives, our ministerial efforts will be successful.

In the wider society, Quicksilvers need us to be their advocates. They are in the most misunderstood developmental stage of life. They need advocates who are committed to their worth and who understand that they seek autonomy and the independence that is only achieved through a personal search for the roots that give identity.

**A Story about Jesus, age 12**
Once upon a time a mother and father journeyed to Jerusalem as was their custom. They took their 12-year-old son with them and when it was time for their return home they discovered him missing. His parents thought he was with relatives, since it was not uncommon for the children to join their kin on long journeys.

After searching and not finding him among the relatives, they returned to Jerusalem. Three days later they found him in the temple, the holiest place in this great city. He was sitting among the elders who were amazed at his maturity. He joined the teachers and began discussing the great questions of life. He displayed remarkable wisdom in his answers and insights as he talked with the leaders about learning, and questioned them about God and God's activity in the world.

His mother approached him with typical parental agitation. Her child had been missing for three days! She was relieved to find him safe, but did not understand his decision to remain behind without permission. She questioned him as was her right and responsibility.

His answers were irritatingly honest. He was about the business of discovering who he was, in relation to his faith group, in relation to other significant adults, and in relation to his God whom he called Abba. And his mother, respecting her child's right to be who God created him to be, kept her opinions to herself.

Thereafter Jesus grew steadily in wisdom and age and grace before God.

In this story we hear our own story as we minister with young adolescents. We will meet the challenge by allowing the Quicksilvers in our midst to be who they are created to be, a people whose identity is best discovered in relationship to God.